Our West Berlin
Storybook From The Island

Our West Berlin

Storybook From The Island

Andreas Austilat, Bernd Matthies, Detlef Kurth, Erkan Arikan, Eva C. Schweitzer, Frank Noack, Gerd Nowakowski, Gretchen Dutschke, Harald Jähner, Harald Martenstein, Ingo Lamberty, Kerstin Schilling, Martina Schrey, Mary Pepchinski, Paul F. Duwe, Paul Hockenos, Ralph Blumenthal, Rosa von Praunheim, Sharona Legner-Zuriel, Tanja Dückers, Ulli Kulke, Uwe Rada, Wladimir Kaminer, and The Südost-Express

New York and Berlin, 2023

Berlinica

Our West Berlin
Storybook From The Island

Authors:
Andreas Austilat, Bernd Matthies, Erkan Arikan, Eva C. Schweitzer, Frank Noack, Gerd Nowakowski, Gretchen Dutschke, Harald Jähner, Harald Martenstein, Ingo Lamberty, Kerstin Schilling, Martina Schrey, Mary Pepchinski, Paul F. Duwe, Paul Hockenos, Ralph Blumenthal, Rosa von Praunheim, Sharona Legner-Zuriel, Tanja Dückers, Ulli Kulke, Uwe Rada, Wladimir Kaminer and The Südost-Express

Editor: Eva C. Schweitzer
Copy Editor: Lia Frances Rockey
Translators: Cindy Opitz, Carolyn Steinberg, Katharina Austilat
Cover: Gerhard Seyfried

165 W 83rd St, New York, NY, 10024

ISBN in the USA: 978-1-935902-54-6
ISBN in Germany: 978-3-96026-067-7
ISBN B&N: 978-3-96026-068-4
LCCN: 2023943795

Printed in the United States and the EU

https://berlinica.com/

Contents

Page

The First Brick in The Wall

By Ralph Blumenthal

FOUR WEEKS BEFORE the Berlin crisis broke last summer, there was nothing in the West Berlin atmosphere to suggest an awareness of what was coming. The sun was hot, the tans were deep, the clothes were bright and fashionable and the people seemed happy and healthy.

They would not say they were afraid of their landsmen, on the east side of the Brandenburg Gate. "It is only politics which separates us," they said. "Besides, how can one be afraid every day for twelve years? You get tired of fear."

Kurfürstendamm, the main West Berlin artery, nicknamed "Kudamm" by the practical Germans, confidently stretched its two miles of Oriental carpet shops, silversmiths, camera stores and Mercedes Benz showrooms. The fine wares in the glass display cases on the wide sidewalk bespoke the prosperity. The twisted, burnt-out steeple of the Kaiser Wilhelm Gedächtniskirche dominating the east end of the Kudamm has come to be accepted by the people and they even tell visitors that they keep it as a warning to themselves.

But the historic German characteristics haven't changed. The first German I met was on the train from Amsterdam. He was a blond, blue-eyed seven-year-old boy whose father owned a large farm in West Germany. The kid could rattle off production figures like a stormtrooper. When he learned I was an American he couldn't contain his curiosity. "How many men," he wanted to know, "were there in the FBI? Do they wear uniforms? Do they carry guns? Pistols or rifles?"

At the East-West border check, he showed an astounding political awareness. Throughout the "orientation" lecture about East Germany that each visitor is compelled to sit through at the border, he shouted "Propaganda!" so loud and continuously that I felt sure the East German police woman would have us all arrested.

The West Germans were not thinking of the next war and they were trying hard to forget the last one: West Berlin helps them forget. The few remaining bomb ruins are rapidly being replaced by modern projects and developments. The mass rowhouses built during the 1930s are being hidden by the newer constructions and therefore stand out less ominously.

But there are still those who can't forget. They are haunted by guilt, troubled by nightmares. When I signed the register in an old but stately rooming house, the landlord looked at my name and, apparently feeling that some sort of explanation was necessary, said to me in German, "I helped many Jews during the war. I kept them here. I did."

The East Berliners seemed no more aware of the impending crisis than their western brothers. However, it is harder for them to forget the last war. About fifty per cent of the Soviet sector is still in ruins.

The East Berlin counterpart of the Kudamm is Stalinallee, formerly Frankfurter Allee. Although its shops don't approach those of the Kudamm with respect to quality merchandise and luxuries, the avenue itself is monumental, each wide sidewalk being divided by a mall with trees. However, through the archways of the impressive facades, the ruins behind are visible.

The West Berliners have constructed an elaborate pleasure dome dedicated to the "laugh, drink and make merry" principle which is another reaction, or non-reaction, to their problems. The name of the nightclub is Resi. Each table there is equipped with a small telephone connecting to the other tables. Those people too shy to call others can send messages to them via pneumatic tubes. When the phones start ringing and the tubes start clicking more than one guest can—for the moment—free himself of the fear that waits outside the door.

I wrote this article in September 1961 when I was beginning my senior year at the City College of New York. As news editor of the student paper, the City College Campus, I assigned myself to report on my junior summer abroad --my first overseas trip. Of course, it included an ancestral visit to Berlin, where my family had deep roots. As I then wrote, Berlin was enjoying a lovely summer—once called "Hitler weather"—with little to suggest the upheaval just around the corner: a hateful Communist wall that would split the city, east and western Europe, and the entire world. Nor did I imagine then how well I would come to know divided Berlin as a foreign correspondent of *The New York Times* in 1968-69, and later as a researcher of my family's happy and tragic history in a reunited city.

My father, Hans Blumenthal, was born in Berlin in the last month of the last year of the 19th century. His two older sisters left Germany in the 1920s as early Zionist settlers in the British mandate of Palestine, establishing flourishing new roots of the family in what was to become Israel. Hans, too, fled home as soon as possible, for reasons I never learned.

Like many patriotic German Jews, he was quick, even at 17, to rally to the fatherland in the Great War, becoming a stretcher-bearer in an ambulance unit on the Western Front. Luckily, he was captured by the British in 1918 and survived the carnage as a POW. His best childhood friend, Szilard Diamant, had a younger sister, Rosa, born in 1902, which is how my father met the love of his life –my mother-to-be -- whom he married in 1929. With enviable foresight, they promptly sailed for the U.S., arriving just in time for the stock market crash and the Great Depression but well before Hitler might have sent them fleeing (or not, too rooted in their homeland to escape the Holocaust.) I grew up in the German-Jewish enclave of Inwood in northernmost Manhattan in the care of my German-speaking Omi, my mother's mother –also a Berliner and, by 1934, a refugee from Nazism. Two of her brothers soon followed.

Like the stupid son in the Passover Haggadah, I didn't ask them enough questions and had to piece together their histories later -- what little I could. I didn't do much digging on my maiden voyage to Berlin, or even a few years later, posted to Bonn as a *Times* correspondent. I arrived just days after the Soviet invasion of Czechoslovakia in August 1968. Germans on both sides of the Iron Curtain were in a panic, along with much of the rest of the world. Would the Russians keep rolling west, triggering World War III? What about divided Berlin, inside the Soviet zone? *Times* bureau chief David Binder suggested I fly back and forth, in case the Russians were shooting down western planes. Great idea, I agreed, but then I might not be the one writing the story.

I did make regular road trips to Berlin and East Germany. Until I was detained for interrogation. In Leipzig, where I'd gone for a twice-yearly trade fair that offered a revealing window on the reclusive Communist bloc, I had written about rare anti-Soviet protests that broke out in the German Democratic Republic after the invasion of Czechoslovakia. My handler had warned me the story wouldn't sit well with the authorities, and it didn't. Then, too, the Volkspolizei had found, crumpled in my wallet, a suspicious slip of paper reading "Rother, antenna." It was a long-forgotten note to ask my Bonn landlord about TV reception, but it reeked of espionage. They finally let me go but from then on, over the protests of my editors and the American embassy, I was barred from Berlin. So when my parents bravely overcame a vow never to return to their homeland and paid me a visit in Bonn, their native city was left off the itinerary.

I didn't get back to Berlin for more than forty years, long after my parents died, the Soviet Union and the wall fell, and Germany reunited. In 2011, I returned to a very different capital city with our two daughters on a roots tour. This time, we visited the apartment building at 49 Guenzelstrasse in the Wilmersdorf section where, I had learned, my mother's extended family had lived since at least 1919. That included my mother's older brother, my uncle Szilard, and his wife, Hella, from Oswiecim (Auschwitz to the Germans) until 1939 when, his metals business having been been "Aryanized" and his Czech residency papers having expired, they fled to Slovakia.

That's where they were rounded up in 1942 and put aboard trains to the east, Szilard to disappear, murdered enroute or in Majdanek or Bergen-Belsen, or who-knows-where?, and Hella to land in a Sobibor work camp from which she miraculously managed to escape, surviving the war with fake Catholic papers in Warsaw and emigrating to Australia in the 1950s with a new husband and stepson.

Having pieced together that much more of my family history, I returned to Berlin once again in 2015, this time with my wife, to re-visit 49 Güntzelstrasse and lay Stolpersteine for Szilard and Hella, a story I was to tell in *The New York Times*, "In Berlin, Unraveling a Family Mystery."

Ralph Blumenthal, a Distinguished Lecturer at Baruch College of the City University of New York, was an award-winning reporter for The New York Times *from 1964 to 2009. He has written and co-authored seven books on organized crime and cultural history. He co-authored a series of groundbreaking* Times *articles on the secret Pentagon program to investigate UFOs. Photo: Deborah Blumenthal*

The Day When Kennedy Came

By Gerd Nowakowski

When John F. Kennedy visited West Berlin in the summer of 1963 and announced "Ich bin ein Berliner" in front of the City Hall, the city not only caught the world's attention, but this statement also brought West Berliners together. Many of them were on their feet to see the American President; one of them was the thirteen-year-old Gerd Nowakowski.

"Sunny with only a very slight chance of rain" is the weather forecast for June 26, 1963. The weather is splendid on the Wednesday of the American President's visit, which has kept the walled city in feverish expectation for days. Inappropriate, it seems to some, is the wording in the weather report: "The increase in air pressure in recent days has brought Germany into the no-man's-land between two fronts," says *Der Tagesspiegel*. We react sensitively to such words; after all, we live in the "frontier town." But here we are dealing with completely different fronts: low pressure Melusine hangs over the North Sea; and over Warsaw, far to the east, is the core of a high pressure area.

Warsaw, that's unimaginably far away for the 13-year-old schoolboy, and not just this Wednesday. At Checkpoint Charlie, behind that white line on Friedrichstrasse, still in no-man's-land, he and his friends know their way around. And this visit is a change from everyday school life. Maybe no-man's-land was not the correct term—the few yards in front of the ugly Wall topped with barbed wire actually already belonged to East Berlin.

But soldiers from the East Berlin side rarely came to inspect the Wall. Behind the Wall was the dangerous zone, with powerful searchlights illuminating the death strip, cleared of plant life. The West Berlin police did not dare to patrol the shadow of the Wall either. The boy and his friends had been to this no-man's-land before, and the smaller boys had watched the older ones pompously light a cigarette.

Today, the boy is here again. All students in the walled city are off school. Now, thousands of people are standing here, cheering for a man a hundred yards away on a white-painted dais, looking east over the Wall. It's a good thing that the dais is elevated. Otherwise, the 13-year-old would not have been able to see the U.S. president in the middle of the crowd. The boys have found their place in the narrow

strip between the Wall, whose slabs and stones are so roughly and carelessly jointed that the mortar is oozing out, and the only house that the war has left standing. The pharmacy "Zum Weißen Adler" is located on the ground floor.

The boys have a couple of cardboard signs with them, made in class. "Welcome, Mr. President," they have written carefully in white ink. The 13-year-old has nailed his sign to a piece of roughly planed square timber. It's so long that he can stretch it up into the sky far above his head so that the guest doesn't miss it. The wood is planed so roughly that a splinter drills into his hand. That hurts. But it doesn't bother him. He wants to see the man who is like a movie star to him and his friends. A man from another world, the USA. None of the boys have ever been there, they can't even imagine such a trip. Many afternoons after school they stand by the fence at Tempelhofer Feld where the American Air Force planes take off and land, and imagine where the pilots fly to. For the boys, the USA is as far away as the moon that the Americans want to conquer; they've already sent half a dozen astronauts into space. But all the boys know is that all Americans drive huge cars and have huge refrigerators in their homes. None of their fathers have a car, let alone a road cruiser. Many parents don't even have a refrigerator.

The pharmacy "Zum Weißen Adler," located in the blind spot of world history and which will not close until 1970, is closed today. The corner building looks as though it's only had makeshift repairs, even eighteen years after the war. Still, behind the windows of the upper floors, people are standing and waving at the President.

For days, the police has been checking on residents all over the city, to guarantee the President's security. All tenants have been provided with notices telling them not to let strangers into their apartments. Residents of the house with the pharmacy, who live closer to the dividing line between two world powers than they would like, now have a front row seat. This time, it's for a happy occasion. They can look straight down at the President and at the many camera crews. Journalists are standing on a specially constructed platform, right next to the large sign that reads, "You are leaving the American Sector," printed also in French and Russian.

Shortly after noon, the air is warm as if it is summer. The President has been in West Berlin for three and a half hours. Eight hours are planned for the visit to the divided city, the eastern-most outpost of the democratic world. It's a short time only, but for the Berliners it is the longest eight hours in their history. Every Berliner who was there can still remember this day. John F. Kennedy's visit is burned into West Berlin's collective memory; similar to the night the Wall came down in November 1989, twenty-six years later.

On June 26, 1963, the day of Kennedy's visit, West Berlin was a city whose future was threatened. Fresh in everyone's memory was the blockade of the half-city by the Soviet Union fifteen years earlier. The Western Allies, led by the USA, let hundreds of "candy bombers" fly every day for a year and a half to make sure that the city, sealed off from West Germany, would survive. Since August 13, 1961, when the GDR government had built the inhumane bulwark, with the approval of the Soviet leadership, Berliners had been in a state of mental shock, a collective depression, because nobody knew how things would continue. Many had almost shamefacedly and secretly made their decision, having sold their houses or land, or were in the process of relocating the production of their companies, piece by piece, to the safe Federal Republic of Germany.

Now a President is coming who will give people courage. "John— you our best friend" is written on a poster in somewhat awkward English. After the American head of state lands at Tegel Airport and begins his drive to the city center, hundreds of thousands of Berliners line the streets and cheer for this charismatic President. On the journey through the city, he inscribes himself into the hearts of the people who thirst for encouragement, even before he has delivered that one sentence in front of almost half a million listeners at the Schöneberg City Hall, which is both an incantation and a promise: "Ich bin ein Berliner."

The city has been preparing for the visit for days. Everyone should, and everyone wants, to see the President. All offices and museums remain closed, work is suspended at many companies, the courts work according to an emergency service plan. Garbage collection is canceled, and even the bread rolls are baked earlier because the bakers guild, like the butchers and other grocers, recommends closing the shops at twelve o'clock.

The post offices also have reduced their hours. They have also issued a special postmark with an inscription reading "Visit of U.S. President Kennedy" and the national coat of arms of the USA. The closure of swimming pools in all districts upsets only a few students. They all want to see Kennedy, whose route they have known for days because every newspaper has printed it. All over the city, people have chosen places to get a particularly good view of Kennedy. Some sit on traffic signs or lanterns, cling to fences for hours or have built pyramids out of beer crates to sit on.

The boys at Checkpoint Charlie have already lost their sign welcoming the youthful head of the Western superpower. It has quickly become tiresome for them in the crush of the crowds anyway. In the feverish excitement of the Berliners, which the boy cannot put into words, but which he can feel, all the rules that otherwise apply seem to have been overridden. No adult scolds him when he climbs a lamp-post; even the police only have eyes for the overseas visitor. If you are adventurous enough, you could even walk through the open front doors of the Schöneberg City Hall, climb up to the attic and reach the roof through a hatch.

At Checkpoint Charlie, the President stands at the white line that marks the boundary between the two enemy blocks. He looks across the border into East Berlin, where a few hundred people have gathered far away at the exit of the Stadtmitte subway station. At the Brandenburg Gate, the GDR government uses large tarpaulins to prevent people from looking over there. Now people on Friedrichstrasse are trying to get close to John F. Kennedy, despite the police marching in. The U.S. guest keeps looking east for a few minutes. The President's brother, Robert Kennedy— five years after JFK's assassination he will also fall victim to an attack whose causes are highly disputed— has even briefly put his foot beyond the white line.

So now J. F. Kennedy is in no-man's-land, just like those boys from Kreuzberg who are here every day. At Checkpoint Charlie, the crossing point for foreigners with the small control booth, they can see all the elegant and rare foreign cars that cross the border to the "East Sector." It is exactly the spot where the same boys stood almost two years earlier in August. World history was being written as tanks faced each other: here the American armored tubes pointed "over there," into the Soviet sphere of influence. On the other side, the colossal Soviet tanks stood ready to shoot. At the time, the world held its breath.

In October 1961, the mood at Checkpoint Charlie was depressed. A strange silence could be witnessed, as if any inappropriate noise could trigger an escalation. The boys felt this, too. At the time, the newly elected President John F. Kennedy sent a special envoy, General Lucius Clay, to Berlin— the man who had shown West Berliners once before, during the blockade and the airlift, that the United States was determined not to bow to Soviet leadership.

Now the President himself is standing at Checkpoint Charlie. This is not the time for silence, now is the time for rejoicing. He descends from the viewing platform and walks back about a hundred yards to Kochstrasse, today's Rudi-Dutschke-Strasse, where his motorcade is waiting. And on this journey even his bodyguards finally give up. On his way to the city center, the Secret Service have to repeatedly push away people who have rushed towards the open car to shake Kennedy's hand. Some of them have a toddler on their shoulders or a bouquet of flowers in their hands. A baker's wife tries in vain to hand him a cake into the car.

Here on Kochstrasse, the President himself dives into the crowd and shakes hands with enthusiastic Berliners. Pierre Salinger, the White House press officer and Kennedy confidant, later says that nothing impressed the President more than this reception in Berlin. He told him this after his departure.

The President is now in the middle of the crowd, a nightmare for the security-conscious U.S. intelligence squad. The Berlin police officers assigned to cordon off the sidewalk also lose their strict formation; only their white caps still flash in the crowd. Eventually, the President climbs back into his midnight blue Lincoln to continue his triumphal journey. The Berliners let confetti and streamers rain on him.

This emotional state of emergency lasts eight hours—the longest eight hours in the history of Berlin so far. This day buzzes with the endless number of stories that are told in the evening because everyone has experienced something that will survive longer than this day. And so has the 13-year-old boy. Sixty years later, Berliners still know exactly where they were on that day.

Gerd Nowakowski was born and raised in Berlin. The mechanical engineer was part of the founding generation of the leftwing daily newspaper taz. *For many years, he was bureau chief in Bonn when the city was the capital of Germany. After the Wall came down, he was the editor of the Berlin Metro section. At* Der Tagesspiegel, *he headed the editorial department as managing editor.* *Photo: Mike Wolff*

Christmas Rituals

By Kerstin Schilling

THERE WAS HARDLY a time with more traditions and rituals in West Berlin than the season of Advent leading into the many days of Christmas. Many of the traditions we experienced in our childhood are still in our life today as we adapt the customs of our family's Christmas into adulthood. And by that, we transform ourselves into our parents, whether we like it or not.

As the children of West Berlin, however, we had two particularly special rituals associated with Christmas, unique to the Walled City. Both left an unforgettable mark on our childhood, but sadly, they were mostly forgotten with the fall of the Wall.

The first ritual was the pre-Christmas visit to family and friends in East Berlin or in East Germany. This was well organized, precisely planned and prepared months ahead. Our parents shopped all around and packed the purchases artfully, filling large bags with oranges and grounded coffee, deodorant and silk stockings. In addition, we packed a few personal gifts.

What we could not put in the bag, however, was books or musical records. This was strictly forbidden by the GDR and any attempt to smuggle any of those could result in long, long waits at the border. Even worse, the Grepos—Grenzpolizisten, border police—would confiscate the bags. In addition, our packages could not be sealed with sticky tape. They were loosely tied so that they could easily be opened for an inspection. This persisted with us long after the fall of the Wall. It had nothing to do with today's ecological considerations, it was simply a deep-seated habit.

Now the next step: Our presents in tow, we went to the nearest border control point. For my family, this was Friedrichstrasse or Bornholmer Strasse in the North. When I was a child, this all seemed so normal to me—I was very surprised to learn that my West German relatives did no such thing. Although they did visit their relatives in East Germany at Christmas, this was never preceded by planning and preparing and packing at such a scale.

We also sent packages to friends in the GDR via postal services. It was not only our parents that did this, most West Berliners joined in. Incredible scenes took place in the post office during Advent, when hundreds of parcels and packages were sent on their way into the "zone," as we called the GDR. At the post office at Bahnhof Zoo, which was open

until after midnight, we witnessed downright riots, especially during the last few minutes. Some families threw their parcels over the partition window where they were skillfully caught by postal workers who kept the crowd at bay with loud shouts.

The shipping of the parcels required preparation and planning as well. But despite all these troubles, we could not imagine the pre-Christmas season without parcels. They were as much a part of Advent as writing Christmas cards before e-mail was invented.

Even after the fall of the Berlin Wall, when we could spontaneously visit family and friends anywhere and at any time without a passport or a permit, our habit of wrapping gifts thoughtfully was still deep-seated, although we were now taping the packages shut. At this point, anyone in East Germany could also buy anything from anywhere. And yet, for a long time, we still felt obligated to bring everyday necessities along when we visited a friend in East Berlin. However, our friends and relatives in the East had now picked up the same habit: they also gave us silk stockings or household goods if they found an affordable opportunity to buy them.

The second important ritual was the candle greeting that shone all the way to East Berlin every Christmas Eve—or, at least, was supposed to shine. At that time, most apartments in West Berlin had old wooden, double-paned windows. On Christmas Eve, we would place lit candles between these two panes. This was meant as a greeting to the people in the eastern part of our city. Those illuminated windows were a sign that they had not been forgotten. And it didn't matter whether our relatives in the East could actually see the candles or not.

In my family—and probably in most families in West Berlin—the candle ceremony went like this: We used small shot glasses to serve as candleholders. A white household candle or a small Christmas tree candle was fixed to the bottom of the glass with hot wax. Then we placed several of these makeshift candlesticks between the two windows, all of them already lit.

There was no set time for that ritual, but six o'clock in the evening seemed suitable to us. The old double windows were never quite tight, so there was always a draft inside. The candles dripped a lot, became lopsided, and burned down quickly. But this did not bother us, because the purpose was fulfilled. The greeting to "over there" had been sent. The fact that we children had to scrape the wax residue off the window sill the next morning was also part of the Christmas rituals. And, of course, the candles were a sign of the impending gifts on Christmas Eve.

For us children, the placing of the candles was associated with solemnity. But for a long time, we did not understand the significance this gesture had for our parents and grandparents, especially at that early time when visits to East Berlin were not even possible. We considered it a customary part of Christmas Eve and did not worry about who could actually see the candles burning briefly in an apartment on the mezzanine. Today I understand that this ritual was soothing for the generation of my parents and grandparents who could not see or meet their family and friends, or could do so only with great difficulty.

Otherwise, the Christmas season had the advantage of emptying Berlin of people. The many West Germans who had moved in were no longer in the city. Even hard-boiled leftists and Christmas despisers among the left-wing students in the pre-war districts went "home" to their parents for the festive season. And they usually had no relatives in East Germany to visit or give presents to.

Kreuzberg, Neukölln and Schöneberg were particularly emptied out during the holidays, since all of the leftish-liberal West German students returned to their parents to eat their fill of roast goose and stollen, gaze at the Christmas tree, meet friends and tell them all about their adventures in Berlin. And despite all of their criticism of consumerism and capitalism, they dutifully accepted their parents' gifts. After they returned to West Berlin, those gifts were frequently shown off in their favorite counter-culture Kreuzberg pub, and often fiercely discussed.

We, the real Berliners, were occasionally ridiculed for not leaving town for Christmas. On the other hand, we enjoyed the fact that we didn't have to make the long journey to the boondocks, rather cumbersome by train as well as by carpool; or very expensive by air. But in the end, we were just as parochial with our family ceremony as they were. We certainly felt as well that we were competing with the West Germans for "cosmopolitanism."

Those gifts from the West German parents, however, were not always met with the desired response. This was mainly due to the fact that this parental generation had lost their connection to the Wall city. For many of them, West Berlin lay just outside the Soviet Union. Their perception was shaped by the Berlin airlift, the Federal subsidies, and by the even more plentiful scathing reports in the tabloids about civil unrest and troubles in the Walled City. They saw no reason why this juggernaut was pampered in the first place. And many parents were not happy that their children were living in dingy areas with squatters, punks, and Russians right outside the door.

When their children spent Christmas in the West German idyll, many parents tried to be "helpful." I remember a friend whose parents had won a car in a lottery. Yes, there was such a thing in those days! Overjoyed, they took this as an occasion for an extraordinary Christmas present, because—as they had announced publicly—their poor daughter in the walled city did not own a car. At those times, this was completely incomprehensible in Germany, in the countryside as well as in any city. So the car arrived in West Berlin, presumably by tortuous routes.

However, the daughter was a professional musician. At that time she was engaged in establishing a counter-cultural, all-female band. She sold the car right away and used the money to acquire a high-quality saxophone to further her career as a musician. She continued to travel to gigs and rehearsals with the new instrument by subway or on her bicycle. As her parents found out, they withdrew from their own daughter in shock. I continued to make music with her and the new saxophone for a few years until we parted ways. The instrument surely lasted longer than the car.

This was all a long time ago. Since then, Advent and Christmas rituals have changed, as has all of West Berlin. West and East Berliners have mixed. There is the unifying element of Berlin origins. But at the same time, if you meet a new acquaintance, there is still a quick check of where the other person is from. Only recently, I mentioned living in Schöneberg to a colleague still in her thirties and she remarked, "Ah, the other Berlin." I almost put up a candle in amazement....

Today, the candles are no longer necessary, as we now can celebrate with those we once only greeted from afar. Many double windows have been replaced by modern windows, aluminum, and soundproof. Also, app-controlled LED lights would probably be used today if the lighting ritual still existed. And today, when the once revolutionary Kreuzbergers—or Prenzlauer Bergers—still leave the city for their parents' house, they install variable lighting systems to fool potential burglars into thinking that the apartment is occupied over the holidays.

We former children of West Berlin only occasionally harbor sentimental thoughts about the glowing window candles. However, the power the symbol still has is shown by the strings of lights and rows of candles that are often used today as a greeting of peace or friendship.

Most recently, candles were placed in the windows for the victims of the attacks on the Christmas markets at Breitscheidplatz in Berlin and Strasbourg in 2019. It is a sign of solidarity and a tradition that has survived to the present day.

Kerstin Schilling was born in the Berlin district of Reinickendorf in 1962 and has spent almost her entire life in West Berlin. She published Happy Island—Generation West Berlin. *As a cultural manager, she has worked in East and West Germany, in both parts of the city, and in France. Since 2012, her office was in Potsdam, but her residence is in the district of Schöneberg.* *Photo: private*

PAN AMERICAN
WORLD AIRWAYS

The Course Of the Air

By Bernd Matthies

How did y'all ever endure it back then in West Berlin, with it being enclosed by the Wall? Let's answer it this way: free air travel helped us, but it was more of a symbolic option than a practical one. This was due to high airfares and the fact that we were used to perceiving the journey by car via the transit Autobahn through the GDR as an excruciating but nevertheless reliable method of travel. Flying was something for the rich, for businessmen and politicians.

How did I come to take my first flight? The reason is directly related to the political situation in Berlin. But it's complicated. Some West Berliners had to avoid setting foot in East German territory because, for example, they had helped to get refugees out of the GDR, were politically far to the right, or belonged to the Christian Democratic Party in exile. That party consisted of members had fled or been expelled from the SBZ— Sowjetische Besatzungszone, Soviet Zone of Occupation—, as the GDR was initially called. If they wanted to take a vacation, they had to fly.

But vacationing without your own car was not an option back then; rental cars were practically non-existent or only available for hair-raising prices. So how did your car follow suit? The car would be registered to an unsuspicious straw man and driven through the GDR by said straw man. Of course, the car often changed hands in Hanover, Hamburg or Nuremberg, because the straw driver had to return somehow, and in good time. Returning by train was an option, but the trains were not only controlled by the GDR, they were also extremely slow because of these controls. So, some drivers were reluctant to ride it.

That's how I got on my first flight, which must have been around 1960: My father, politically unsuspicious, ferried a suspicious friend's car to West Germany and took me along as an escort. We flew back to Berlin from Hanover in a humming DC-6 operated by PanAm (at that time,

Berlin was controlled by the four Allies of World War II and only their airlines were allowed to serve the city). Our flight went without any particular incident. My father smoked on board, as it was customary then, and the staff served a sandwich to each of us. The flight was a bit rough, because the altitude in the corridors was limited to nine thousand feet, a little less than two miles. On many of those flights the plane rode the crests of the clouds and ran into any turbulence available.

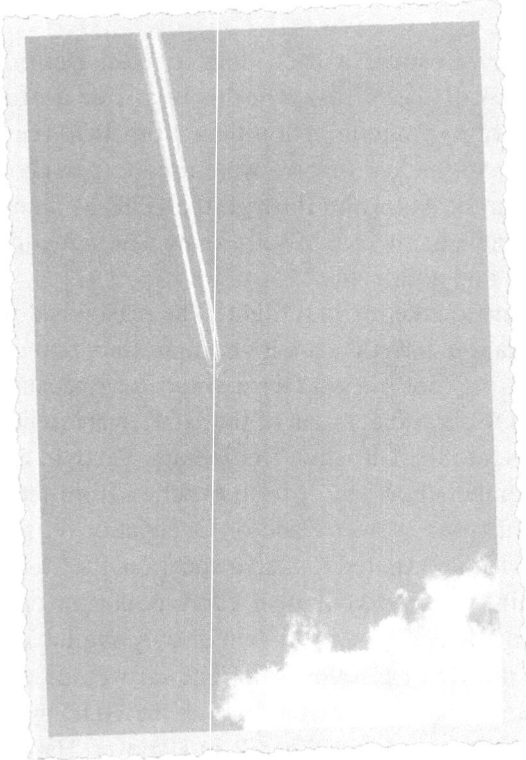

Sometime later, I ended up in Munich, at the old Riem airport, also during bad weather. Today, the airsickness bags are kept only as a reminder, but in those days they turned out to have some practical purpose, especially on those somewhat longer routes. It's unlikely that anyone has ever compiled statistics on this politically induced domestic German air tourism, but we were pretty sure that it was not without economic significance, especially on the short routes.

In those old times, flying had the aura of the unfamiliar, the luxurious, even if it was only to Hannover-Langenhagen and not to Singapore or Antigua. Even folks who weren't planning to take off themselves could at least press their noses against the glass windows at Tempelhof—because anyone could get right up all the way to the gate without controls.

Tempelhof was the legendary central city airport, conceived in the Golden Twenties, the place where candy bombers landed during the

blockades in 1948 and 1949, and where Cold War movies such as Billy Wilder's One, Two, Three and Octopussy with James Bond were shot. Despite its age, Tempelhof had the aura of modernity early on. Airport managers continued to cultivate it after the war, with fancy baggage carousels and little things like the first automatic doors in the city, which were opened by a little kick; motion detectors had not yet been invented.

Just after World War II had ended, the Allies put also Tegel airport into operation, and managed to do so after only ninety days of construction. However, the highly effective, much-loved hexagonal terminal building that gave access to all gates within a relatively small space was not built until around 1970. With Tegel, the desire to fly slowly took hold within the general population. On the other hand, in the wake of the transit agreement between West Germany and the GDR, the perceived threat at the border checkpoints declined; hardly anyone had to take the detour through the air any more.

With the easing of tensions, it wasn't only political customs that loosened in West Berlin, but also attitudes toward flying. At first, prices in Tegel remained uncomfortably high, but suddenly low-cost carriers popped up: Eastern Bloc airlines like Interflug opened up the world from Schönefeld, the airport in East Berlin, and for relatively little money.

Let's say they flew to destinations east of Berlin, albeit this explicitly included Rome, Athens and further afield. Bookings were made through West Berlin travel agencies, which then also opened up access to Schönefeld, comparatively free from red tape. Buses ran nonstop from the Tempelhof train station to Schönefeld.

Until the fall of the Wall, Schönefeld flights were quite popular in West Berlin. They were also a source of precious Western currency for the East.

The border checks were relatively quick, but you still had to allow a significant amount of time for them, and those pesky guards were also quite annoying. Probably only the natives of West Berlin who were hardened by travelling the transit Autobahn could endure them. Also the flight itself could be longwinded. For example, if you flew with the Hungarian airline Malev from Schönefeld to Rome, you couldn't avoid a stopover in Budapest. On the other hand, that was a good occasion for an overnight stay in a dusty hotel including chicken paprika and a Puszta band.

Occasionally, however, the guards would let things slide. A colleague once traveled to Istanbul via Schönefeld, and as a precaution she carried two passports with her (in case one of them was stolen); a West Berlin passport and a West German passport, which the East German authorities did not recognize on principle. After all, they saw West Berlin as an "independent political entity" whose residents were not allowed to have a West German passport. After the return flight, she unfortunately presented the wrong passport, the one that had been not been stamped on the outward flight. The border guard said, calmly: "Well, why don't you check if you have another passport somewhere in your bag." When it came to Western currency, the GDR could be surprisingly free of ideology.

However, Schönefeld was never really popular with West Berliners, especially since its interior was as confusing and impenetrable as that of the border crossing at the Friedrichstrasse train station—and like there, the entire shopping area consisted of one single Intershop, which was mostly popular with smokers, due to tax-free cigarettes. Schönefeld has hardly changed all the way up to 2020, although there were persistent rumors of lofty plans for a new airport. But that is a completely different story.

Bernd Matthies, born in 1953, learned to read at elementary school in the district of Tempelhof, where he grew up, and to write at the Henri Nannen School for Journalism in Hamburg. Since 1983, the journalist has worked in various capacities for the Berlin daily paper Der Tagesspiegel, *where he still writes satirical pieces, essays, commentaries and restaurant reviews.* *Photo: private*

The Blue Angel is Coming Home

By Frank Noack

THE LAST TIME Marlene Dietrich set foot close to her birthplace was January 1964, two and a half years after the Wall had gone up. The Hollywood star was changing planes at the East Berlin airport Schönefeld from Paris on her way to a performance in Warsaw. Suddenly, she saw herself surrounded by local journalists. A reporter from *Neues Deutschland,* the main East German Communist paper, asked her: Did she know that *Judgment at Nuremberg*, the last movie in which she had starred, was running in East Germany with great success? No, Marlene said, and she did not care. The only thing on her mind was the upcoming concert in Poland. She remained polite, but the atmosphere, caught on film, is chilly.

Marlene was a dedicated anti-Fascist, but first of all a cosmopolitan, so she might have distrusted the provincial communist definition of anti-Fascism. Even though she performed all over West Germany, and in far-flung places like Sao Paolo and Tokyo, and despite some half-hearted negotiations for a concert at Friedrichstadt Palast, she never appeared on a stage in the East. But why? There is some evidence that she was put off by the lurid East German reports on her German tour of 1960 that was panned as disastrous in Communist papers — and that would become part of how she is remembered.

Marlene's relationship with Berlin, West Berlin really, was complicated; a "love-hate affair," as the actress herself once said. She was worshipped and adored in her hometown, yet also booed and attacked. But Berlin was always in her heart. She lived to see the reunification of Berlin; two years later, on May 6, 1992, she died, ninety years old, in Paris, lonely and sick. She had not left her bedroom for five years. But she was buried close to her birthplace in a small cemetery steps away from her mother Josephine.

Marlene's funeral is nearly as glamorous as her life. At 10.30 am, an open black Cadillac arrives at the gate of the cemetery, escorted by dozens of police cars. The car carries her coffin, which was flown in from Paris by Lufthansa a few days earlier. At the Berlin funeral home, the coffin is rigorously guarded — intruders had already tried to break into the Paris parlor. The small cemetery is cordoned off the previous night, but in the morning, hundreds of mourners crowd the entrance. They applaud, throw flowers, and call her name. Marlene!

Approximately one hundred guests are invited: Marlene's daughter Maria Riva and her grandchildren, but also local politicians. Berlin's mayor Eberhard Diepgen is among them, a few diplomats—Americans and French— and a handful of longtime old actor friends, most importantly Maximilian Schell and Hildegard Knef. More than four hundred members of the press are put on a stand, one hundred fifty feet away.

Hanna Schygulla, the grande dame of German cinema, remembers Marlene fondly. "We, the ones born afterward, the postwar generation, are proud that there were people like you, people who during the Hitler period took the side of the enemy, and did it out of love for a better Germany," Hanna says. "Marie Magdelene Dietrich is dead, but Marlene Dietrich remains. The Blue Angel does not die."

Marie Magdalene was Marlene's name when she was born in a neighborhood nicknamed Red Island—red, because it was communist, and island, because it is surrounded by the tracks of the S-Bahn. It is part of Schöneberg, only steps to the place where David Bowie would eventually move to. Her last movie, *Just a Gigolo*, starred Bowie (but, sadly, was a flop). She became an actress in the Golden Twenties in Berlin. In 1930, she had her breakthrough with *The Blue Angel,* where she played Lola, the seductive nightclub singer. She moved to Hollywood and starred in movies that created her image of romance, eroticism, and mystery.

But Marlene's final return was not been welcomed all over Berlin. Local paper got letters from disgruntled Berliners who thought of her as a traitor, undeserving of a public funeral. "What has this woman ever done for Berlin?" one of them asked. "While we were living in poverty and misery, she was enjoying the high life abroad." And another one scolded: "She made tons of money in America, why is she not buried over there."

One hour has passed at the cemetery, where a Lutheran minister presides over the funeral. He reads the 23rd Psalm. "The Lord is my shepherd; I shall not want. He maketh me to lie down in green pastures: he leadeth me beside the still waters." The pastor then moans that Marlene "was often not understood in her beloved homeland." Then Schell reads the poem 'Love as long as you can' by Hermann Ferdinand Freiligrath. After that, Marlene's daughter Maria blows a kiss to her grave.

The cemetery is guarded by the police. The city fears disruptions by right-wingers because of Marlene's anti-Nazi background. But nothing happens. However, Mayor Diepgen is booed. Many Berliners blame him for the failure to organize a tribute at Deutsches Theater, the stage once run by Max Reinhardt where Marlene began her career. Why did the ambitious plans fail? Were stars like James Stewart and Billy Wilder invited on too short notice? Was it sheer incompetence on the part of the city? Or did Diepgen drag his feet because a local election was coming up and he did not want to alienate conservative voters?

Shortly after noon, the guests, the politicians and the family leave. Now ordinary Berliners can step up for a tribute to Marlene. A trail that lasts for more than three hours is forming. Some are carrying white lilies, her favorite flower. They are piling up on the coffin.

Many are signing the condolence book at the entrance. Many admirers are gay or lesbian, but also grandmothers as old as Marlene herself are in line, small kids in tow. Whoever did not make it, could watch the funeral from a pizzeria across the road; it was broadcasted live by Berlin largest TV station, Sender Freies Berlin.

The fallout between Marlene and Berlin goes back to 1933, to the beginning of the Nazi dictatorship. Marlene was in Hollywood, filming another Joseph von Sternberg movie after *The Blue Angel*. Joseph Goebbels, the Nazi-Minister of Propaganda, asked her to come back. She rebuffed him firmly. Eventually, she became an American citizen. And not just that: While Berlin was bombed, she traveled on behalf of the

USO to entertain American soldiers and to encourage them to fight the Nazi army. Some older Germans have never forgiven Marlene for that. In 1960, when the actress visited Berlin for the first time after the war, she faced threats, and once even a large banner that read, “Marlene, Go Home.” In Düsseldorf, a man threw a raw egg at her (however, he nearly got lynched by the audience). When she left, she vowed never to return to Germany. This how she is remembered.

But did she really? Having left Munich on March 27, the last station of her German tour that began in Berlin and included no fewer than twelve concerts, she guested in Tel Aviv on June 17 and was back in Berlin on July 1, staying at the Hilton. That same evening she hurried to the RIAS radio station to record a few songs. The following year she went to Munich to meet three German friends: the Jewish poet Max Colpet, the flamboyantly gay character actor Hubert von Meyerinck, and silent screen veteran Grete Reinwald. The latter two had stayed and filmed in Nazi Germany, but Marlene kept in touch.

On April 24, 1963 she met Berlin’s mayor Willy Brandt in Paris and assured him how much she loved Berlin. Her final concert on German (alas, West German) soil took place on June 13 that same year. She sang Jacques Brel’s famous song: „Ne me quitte pas,” Don’t leave me, We must forget, All can be forgotten, That has already passed away.

The song had been translated into German by her friend Max Colpet.

Marlene has not left Berlin and Berlin has not left her. The city has put up a plaque with her face in 65 Leberstraße, where she was born, and a sign. It reads: “I am, thank God, a Berliner,” — the title of her autobiography. Her grave is only two miles away, but worlds apart.

Frank Noack, born in Berlin in 1961, is a writer specializing in film history. His latest book, Veit Harlan. The Life and Work of a Nazi Filmmaker *(University Press of Kentucky 2016), was a finalist for the Richard Wall Memorial Award. He has reviewed films for* Der Tagesspiegel, Rheinische Post, *and* Siegessäule, *and is also the author of* Emil Jannings. Der erste deutsche Weltstar *(2012).* *Photo: Private*

Little America

By Sharona Legner-Zuriel

THE USUAL WAY to school for most German students from a young age was by foot or by public transportation. My daily mode of transportation was, however, using a school bus supplied by the U.S.-Army. Even more unusual was having an armed U.S.-military police car in front and in back of the bus. But these were the early seventies in West Berlin and the infamous Red Army Faction (RAF), also know as Baader-Meinhof-Group was creating terror across Western Germany. The United States was an enemy and our German-American Community school thus a possible target.

In the Sixties and the Seventies, large areas of Zehlendorf, the south-western, leafy borough of Berlin where our family lived, were the most "Americanized" areas of West Berlin. The American sector had its own housing areas, shopping, a movie theatre, a TV and Radio station, swimming pools, a sports center, a yacht-club, and a golf club.

Our little island in all things American was the German-American Community school or as it was later to be known, the John F. Kennedy School. It had classes all the way from kindergarten to High School or respectively the German Abitur. The school was founded in 1960 by the Senate and the U.S.-Mission in West Berlin. The United States had only a Mission in here, while the U.S. Embassy was in Bonn, the capital of the Federal Republic. The student body consisted of almost fifty percent Germans and Americans respectively, and a small number of pupils from other nations, like myself, a girl with Israeli citizenship.

Today, the school has more than 1500 students from over forty nations on a large, modern campus. But when I enrolled in the early 1960s, we were sitting in make-shift classrooms. While classes were held in German and in English, we could hear various languages in the schoolyard. "Völkerverständigung—International Understanding" was our encompassing motto. We were also the only school not to have classes on Saturday. That meant, school lasted a bit longer during the week, but having a long weekend was definitely worth it. This sounds like a minor issue but was quite forward thinking at the time. Also, our young teachers would sit on their desks during lessons and project work was done in groups. This was also new by Berlin standards, and nearly revolutionary.

Most West Berliners also had never seen a person of color, let alone a full-fledged African American. Again, this was very different in our Little America. Soldiers of color were always present in the streets. And also students and teachers at The Kennedy School had many different ethnic backgrounds. As normal as this is in a multi-cultural city like Berlin today, it was definitely not the norm back then. I remained close with my oldest Black friend Keisha well into adulthood. Sadly, she passed away a couple of years ago.

The heart of our Little America was a shopping mall with super-markets, bakeries, a Brazilian waxing studio and a gym. It was located on Clayallee, one of the main thoroughfares in Zehlendorf, right across from the U.S.-Mission. It was called the PX— Postal Exchange—, and the duty-free shop was reserved solely for members of the U.S. administration in West Berlin, for the Mission and the U.S. Army. Sometime in the 1970s, it was replaced by an even bigger shopping mall called Truman Plaza.

Lucky me, I had an eligible American friend who could shop for me at said Postal Exchange. It was my bestie Allison, or rather, her mom. She would supply marshmallows for the S'mores we would make on a campfire in our backyard. Since we were kids, we are also talking about very "important" American items such as Cool Aid (yes, we did love the artificial taste and it had to be grape flavor which colored our tongue purple) or peanut butter. That was not available in the supermarkets of West Berlin at the time.

We also listened to AFN, American Forces Network. AFN Radio could be heard on any AM receiver. Watching American Television, however, required a TV set with specific technical requirements. And those devices were hard to get. I remember my family holding on to some really old TV that gave us a black and white, grainy picture of AFN TV after hours trying to position our antenna just right. The sound was not great either.

But never mind the bad picture and the awful sound, I faithfully watched my favorite show *Murphy Brown*. My parents, however, were not interested in anything on AFN. I'm not sure what happened first: the final collapse of our old TV set or the end of AFN Television. I just remember that it was suddenly gone and I missed it dearly.

This brings me to another childhood memory: The "Deutsch-Amerikanisches Volkfest". Every summer for two weeks, the German-American Fair" attracted tens of thousands of visitors, including me. I loved rides such as rollercoasters, Ferris wheels, go-carts, and the tunnel of horror. But those, we could have found at any fair in Germany. The highly anticipated American contribution was the food; stands with burgers, hot dogs and corn on the cob, American ice cream and soft drinks like Dr. Pepper and Mountain Dew.

In addition, we enjoyed line dancing, not necessarily the most famous Rock Bands and lots and lots of country music. The latter was not very popular among us younger people, but it still had a big following among visitors who came dressed head to toe in western styled gear. Cultural appropriation was not a thing at that time, so I also saw a lot of white Berliners dressed as American Indians, complete with feather gear and tomahawk.

The other big yearly event was Halloween! The Ghostly Night of Horror is known all over Germany today, but when I was young, it was celebrated strictly in the American sector only. Houses were elaborately decorated with carved pumpkins, skeletons were waving in the wind. And, of course, we were super excited to go "trick or treating" in our more or less scary costumes. My favorite outfit was a raggedy witch with my face painted green—big hat and everything. The loot consisting of the desirable American treats was equally important to us.

Leading a life so different from the other denizens of West Berlin was rather unusual, but it was for a reason. Both of my parents had been refugees from the Nazi regime. My German father had–due to my smart grandfather—left Germany in the early 1930s already for England where he became a citizen. From England, he went to what is now Israel and was then called Palestine.

My Czech-born mother escaped on the so-called "Kindertransport" in 1939, right before the war. The Kindertransport was organized by a member of the British Chamber of Commerce to England and organized by the Quakers. The Quakers found foster families in Great Britain for endangered Jewish children from countries like Germany, Czechoslovakia, or Poland. As the foster families vouched for these children, visas were relatively easy to obtain.

My mother later became a British citizen. After the war, my parents met in Israel and got married. Soonafter, I was born. My father, a lawyer specializing in restitution cases for German Jews, returned with his family to Berlin to set up office here. What was meant to be a brief interlude of two to three years turned out to be a permanent situation. In addition to being British and Israeli citizens, the whole family had German citizenship. But due to their history, all things too "German" did not sit well with my parents. We grew up bilingual and with a strong leaning towards America and Great Britain.

So many things that are now part of German daily life were introduced by the U.S. forces in Germany, and especially in West Berlin. One of them was the "Outpost" theater, also part of the American Sector at Clayallee. It showed films in the American original and solely for moviegoers from the USA. Luckily, some Americans would take their German friends. I was part of a girly group of four BFFs—two Germans, two Americans—and we would watch whatever RomCom or straight up comedy was playing.

For most moviegoers, however, the main attraction was popcorn, something completely unknown in Berlin cinemas back then. At the "Outpost", it only came in the salted variety and lots of it ended up on the floor. It was a snack I definitely didn't like even then and still don't. Sorry. However, I loved the endless choice of candy bars. While we could buy Milky Way and Mars in German supermarkets early on, brands like Baby Ruth or Reeses Peanut Butter were not available.

Of course, all of them were way too sweet and sugary, but we simply desired them for being elusive outside of this secluded world.

In our semi-U.S. enclave, we most certainly lived a sheltered existence. Rugged districts like Kreuzberg or Neukölln seemed far away. And unless you left Berlin on the transit highway through East Germany, you never really saw the Wall. West Berlin (or as the GDR called it: "The independent political entity Westberlin") was located in the middle of the East German state. This created an interesting scenario, but I figured this out only during my college years, which I spent in Kansas.

Corn Country was a strange place for a Berlin girl to go to college, for sure. But my very best friend Gloria went at that time. And it was very important for me to stay together, especially as we practically shared a closet. More importantly, the college recruiter started me as a sophomore already, due to my Abitur. That saved a whole year of tuition.

I made friends in Kansas, and I invited one of them, Kelly, to visit me in West Berlin. She had never left America before, so this was a big trip for her. Her parents looked Berlin up on a map, realized it was located smack in the middle behind the iron curtain and had more than mild reservations to let her travel. It took a lot of convincing from me and my parents and mentioning of Allied troops in the city for her parents to relent.

The most visible sign of Allied troops was the almost daily procession of tanks rolling through the streets. As they regularly passed our school traveling from one army barracks to another, we would stand and wave to them if we were on the playground. Sometimes soldiers would wave back. Nothing sinister here for us children, tanks were simply a daily routine. U.S. soldiers also brought sports such as American football and baseball to West Berlin—the German baseball league was founded in 1957. My two sons still played baseball on a specially designated area, before the city turned it into a housing area.

When we became older, we became quite critical of American global politics. The Vietnam War played a big part in our perception of the USA. Siblings and relatives of American friends were drafted and sent off to war. Liberal minded teachers at our school talked to us about the conflict. That helped shape our perception of an unjust war. More than once, we demonstrated peacefully. I remember a friend and myself walking in circles outside the U.S.-Mission with a placard "Stop the

War"—all under the watchful eye of my father standing on the side lines. He supported our cause, but he was not going to let his young daughter get into trouble with either German or U.S. Police by behaving badly, throwing stones or anything as such.

During that time, we had entered high school already. Our desire to use the protected school bus faded. And the military police decided it was safe enough again to let our buses drive without their presence. As young adults, we preferred the freedom of using public transportation anyway. Freedom to form our own opinions and to view the world from a different viewpoint had shaped our upbringing in this "bubble" of West Berlin.

Even today as alumni from John F. Kennedy school we refer to our group as "JFKler". We still meet from time to time and we still know that what we had was unusual. My very special memory: I still retain some playground gravel in my left knee, from when I fell and scraped it open in elementary school. The scar faded over the years and my memory has never been that good. So, this text also relied on little stories as told by friends. Thank you for your help.

Sharona Legner-Zuriel was born in Haifa, Israel in 1955 and grew up in West Berlin. After a foray into law, she wrote for Volksblatt Berlin *and* Berliner Morgenpost. *She worked for the* Quadriga-*award, the Hasso Plattner Forum, and* new formats. *She was married to journalist Johann Legner, they have two sons. In August 2023, one day before her 68th birthday, she passed away in Berlin. Photo: Studio Urbschat.*

Kids of Kreuzberg

By Detlef Kurth

Right before my birth, in 1966, my parents decided to move to Kreuzberg, the south-eastern, remote half of the borough, called SO 36 by its denizens, after the postal delivery district. My parents were warned: the working-class district was not befitting their status. But that's exactly why they wanted to go there: they were young and left-wing and wanted to change the world. Kreuzberg became our home—a colorful, rough, but also warm home.

In those post-war years, SO 36 was gray and deserted. The city of Berlin was in the process of buying up and clearing out many old tenements in order to build a inner-city highway right where Oranienstrasse runs. A fatalistic mood had taken hold in SO 36. Many residents had been transferred to the sprawling high rises of Märkisches Viertel or Gropiusstadt, and those who moved here were poor or foreign and did not want to stay long: students, Turks, dropouts.

THE PARK. Our lifeline was bus line 28. A line that symbolized SO 36, zigzagging along the wall with no clear direction. Our stop was Lohmühleninsel, an island surrounded by the wall on three sides. We lived on the fourth floor of a stately pre-war building, with hardwood floors and high ceilings. It's hard to believe, but back then such houses were considered inferior. We had two balconies from which we could look into East Berlin twice: to the right into Mitte, where we saw City Hall and the TV tower towering over everything, and to the left into Treptower Park. During the time of the Wall, both were unattainably far away and yet so close.

On Lohmühlen Island, where the Landwehr Canal branches off from the Spree River sat the lock keeper's house. It was located in the West, but administered by the GDR. The lock keepers who worked there were loyal to the party line and members of the SEW, the Socialist Unity Party of West Berlin. That was a different kind of "left" than what my parents understood. This was Dead End. The wall interrupted Schlesische Strasse, which used to run all the way to Silesia.

Lohmühlen Park was the only green spot in the all-gray Kreuzberg SO 36. We children often explored the Wall in the park. The narrow strip in front of the Wall belonged to the GDR. That was because the Wall was built a few feet behind the actual border so that the East German border guards could repair it from the west side. We children

couldn't see what it looked like behind it—the Wall was nearly ten feet high. But we were able to improve it with graffiti.

BAGHDAD Kreuzberg: If we didn't like our parents' vegetarian sandwiches, we could only buy currywurst with fries at a food cart in our early years. But in the sixties and seventies, many Turkish guest workers moved to SO 36. Temporarily, as many believed at the time. At Schlesisches Tor, the next stop on line 28, was the Baghdad, one of the first kebab restaurants. The inexpensive flatbread with skewered meat and salad was invented in Kreuzberg—Turkey had kebab, but not in bread.

This was our salvation when our parents tried a macrobiotic food experiment, for example—no lie—sauerkraut stew with soy cheese.

When the old Kreuzbergers were moved to Gropiusstadt, the old grocery stores also vanished, but now new Turkish shops opened. They offered delicious bread, pomegranates, figs and dates until late in the evening. They tasted like the south and the Mediterranean.

DANGEROUS DUCKS. The tiny riverside park at the Oberbaum Bridge was the only access to the Spree. We often went there to feed ducks. This was extremely dangerous and also politically complicated because the border was not in the middle of the river but ran along the western bank. If a child fell into the water, the West Berlin fire department was not allowed to help. And before a GDR guard boat arrived, the child had long since drowned.

My parents warned us firmly not to play close to the river bank. But it wasn't until several children had drowned that the city set up call boxes to notify the GDR border guards, so they'd know when it was a small duck-feeder that had fallen into the water and not an escape attempt from the East. There were also embrasures hidden on the bank, through whose slits we could observe the East. They were erected right after the Wall was built, when soldiers in West and East were directly opposite each other. Fortunately, no shots were fired at that time.

In the 19th century, the Oberbaum Bridge was a border already; it was the customs wall for barges coming from the Spreewald. In 1963, two years after the Wall was built, the bridge became the first border crossing point for West Berliners who wanted to go to the East. The elevated Metro train, which had crossed the bridge before World War II, now ended at the elevated station Schlesisches Tor. The elevated train had been destroyed in the war and West Berliners could only get across on foot. But today, the train is running again.

THE KINDERGARTEN. The next stop was at the Protestant church at the intersection of Wrangelstrasse and Manteuffelstrasse. The former church kindergarten was now run by a leftwing parents' initiative, of which my parents were also members. They had converted it into a laboratory for anti-authoritarian, non-violent education. The teachers were Montessori educators who wanted to move away from the authoritarian habits of the fifties. Not only did we learn games where boys and girls were equal, but we also conducted political debates. The church tolerated this, insisting only on the traditional service on Christmas. But my parents thought even this was an indoctrination of us innocent little children. They made sure that, at the very least, no hymns were sung, and no Bible texts were read, except for Noah's Ark.

We preferred to go on trips to likewise left-wing Grips Theater on Hansaplatz, where we sang political songs like: "Who says girls are not smart?" Our group of children grew up politically astute, but we had little knowledge of the Bible. Today we still remember the songs from the Grips Theater. But meanwhile, we learned some basic knowledge of Christian culture. And we also celebrated Christmas, just because of the presents.

THE SCHOOL. Bus 28 next stopped at Lausitzer Platz, at the Emmaus Church, which had lost its staple in World War II. My school, the Heinrich Zille elementary school was here, named after the famous illustrator of the 1920s. It was in a beautiful old brick building with a narrow, gray courtyard. Many students came from Turkey, Greece, Yugoslavia or Italy.

Our main playground was the derelict area of Görlitzer Bahnhof, a long-distance train station that also was destroyed in the war. It was opposite Lausitzer Platz, separated by the elevated train from Schlesisches Tor. The Reichsbahn administration, under the auspices of the GDR, had inherited and demolished the ruins. Trains were no longer running from West Berlin to Görlitz anyway, a city in the southeastern tip of the GDR, inaccessibly far away. After school, we wandered between overgrown tracks and heaps of building materials, despite the danger of being buried under loose stones, until we were chased away by the GDR railway police.

We often visited friends from school who lived at Görlitzer Strasse 74, a large building on the corner with a view of the elevated Metro station named for the long-gone Görlitzer Bahnhof. Their house was half dilapidated, the roof leaked, pigeons nested in the walls. We often wondered why the staircase was so wide and had ornate iron railings, and why our friends' apartment had eight rooms, a salon and a hallway long enough for racing. Only later did we find out that the house had been built for the upper management of the Görlitzer Bahn.

This house, like so many others, was emptied out by the municipal company that owned it. Our school friends soon moved away. The turning point came when the citizens' initiative SO 36 squatted the house, led by Volker Härtig, a political activist known all over Kreuzberg. The cartoonist Gerhard Seyfried, who designed the cover of this book, was also among the squatters. Today, the house has been magnificently and expensively renovated, and the abandoned railway site became Görlitzer Park. Are the pigeons still nesting in the house?

In the early 1980s, Mr. Lehmann, a fictional Kreuzberger, arrived at Lausitzer Platz. He was the main character in the novel of the same name written by Sven Regener. The book begins with Mr. Lehmann not daring to walk past a dog. This was completely incomprehensible to us: dogs, along with pigeons and rats, were the only animals we knew. For the Lehmanns, our home was a wellness oasis and a place to get away from it all; they hardly had anything to do with us natives. Actually, their arrival was a sign of the end of the old Kreuzberg as we children knew it.

THE CENTER. At Kottbusser Tor, then as now the center of SO 36, "smart" planners built "New Kreuzberg Center", after they had demolished the Wilhelminian buildings. It was a huge high-rise with balconies reminiscent of sharks. A long-planned city highway was supposed to be added, but fortunately, it never came. The center has almost four hundred units for poor people, as well as a dingy shopping center and a municipal library where we borrowed a book from time to time. The NKZ cordoned off Dresdner Strasse and turned it into a dead end—like all of SO 36.

This didn't just happen to Görlitzer Strasse 74 – tenements were being squatted in all over Kreuzberg. Our parents and us kids thought this was good. We were constantly at rallies, with banners against demolitions and for cheap rents. But sometimes rallies got out of hand.

On May 1, 1987, after a street festival, a still-famous uprising took place around Lausitzer Platz. After a police raid on a squatted building, the black-clad bloc of hard-core leftwingers mounted barricades. Police cars and fire engines were set on fire, shops where looted. At midnight, a Bolle supermarket near Görlitzer Bahnhof burned down completely. Today, a huge mosque is located at this corner.

During these years we constantly attended rallies: for peace, against nuclear power, for the squatters, against the real estate companies and of course against the Senate. At that time, many colorful people had moved to Kreuzberg: punks, freaks, draft dodgers, and orange-clad followers of Bhagwan, the Indian guru. We once saw a punk on Line 28 in full leather gear with a rat on his shoulder. Also organic groceries and bicycle shops opened, self-managed of course, not under the thumb of capitalism. My parents liked it. We found it boring.

THE POOL. The next stop was our summer highlight: Prinzenbad! Swimming, sunbathing, ice cream—we gray-faced kids of Kreuzberg had survived the winter and were enjoying the sun on the green lawn. At that time, apartments were still heated with coal, and unfiltered industrial exhaust gases drifted over from East Berlin. The scratchy air gave us angina, coughs and smog alarms. Curiously, the smog alarm only happened in West Berlin — did the air stop at the Wall?

The Prinzenbad was always overcrowded and there were often brawls among boys. Our sun-deprived skin not only turned red, but also got lots of bruises. At least we learned how to assert ourselves in the smallest of spaces, in the water and on the soon-to-be sun-scorched meadow. We also liked to kick a soccer ball into the middle of a crowd once in a while. But after swimming we were completely docile. That was because we got free entry for collecting garbage on the lawn, so we all eagerly picked up the mess we ourselves had just created.

JUNIOR HIGH. The more bourgeois, western part of Kreuzberg began at Urbanstrasse. This was our stop for High School, from the 7th grade onwards. The school was named after Carl von Ossietzky, the editor-in-chief of the left-wing Weltbühne, who was killed by the Nazis in 1938. Unlike in the traditional Gymnasium, students stayed together until the 10th grade. Many teachers came from the 1968 generation and tried out new teaching methods and new revolutionary insights on us.

Unfortunately, the school had many dark rooms, long dark hallways and air conditioning that prevented the windows from being opened, as well as a crazy color system of green, red and orange that was supposed to deter aggression. For us, it had the opposite effect. Not only did we keep repainting the walls on our own, we also went on strike against dark rooms, air conditioning and soon the asbestos that was discovered everywhere.

THE END. As we grew older, we had no idea what was to come. We thought our insularity, which both protected and constrained us, would last forever. When the Wall came down, we immediately ran to Lohmühlenpark and couldn't believe our eyes: behind the Spree, the green oases of Treptower Park opened up. At first, we believed it was a mirage because we had no idea how huge the park was that had been hidden behind the Wall. And on the northern side, the historic center was revealed with all its magnificent buildings. Today, bus 28, which zigzagged along the wall, has long since disappeared, and so has our old home of Kreuzberg.

Detlef Kurth, born in 1966, studied urban and regional planning at the Techical University Berlin. In 1992, he started working at Planergemeinschaft Berlin and became a research assistant at TU Dortmund soonafter. From 2003 he was a professor of urban planning at HfT Stuttgart and since 2017 at TU Kaiserslautern. He publishes on urban renewal and the turning point of 1989. *Photo: private*

Prison Wine

By Gretchen Dutschke

It was in March 1966 that Rudi Dutschke and I got married and that I moved to Berlin to be with him. Rudi had lived in Berlin since 1961 when he fled the GDR. At that time, early 1966, I read about the commune experiments in the USA. People were moving in together, living in communities, sharing, doing their political work together, or just having fun. I was intrigued and thought, maybe if we did this, if we just lived together and had to face daily life as well as the revolution, we could begin to develop solidarity with each other, especially so women and men could share household tasks, as well as political, theoretical and practical tasks.

From the beginning, I had been shocked by the way men were taking public roles, viewing women as appendages to their boyfriends only. Coming from Chicago, I was not used to the lack of respect toward women that existed among many men in the SDS, the Sozialistischer Deutscher Studentenbund — Socialist Students Union. So I told Rudi about the idea and the hope that I had for it. It would be a new way to enact the revolution. A way that dealt with the means and not just the ends, a way that would lead to a new economic, personal, social and caring society. Maybe it would do away with capitalism as we knew it because it would not be based on ever increasing consumption, but instead on ever increasing solidarity and better personal relationships.

Rudi liked the idea. "You organize it," he said. "We can have a meeting here at our house. We'll invite people for the first meeting."

"I'll invite them, not you," I said.

OK. He agreed.

I wanted to invite only the people that I found to be open to diversity—tolerant and friendly people, no machos. So I made a list of those whom I felt met those qualifications. We invited them. In the days leading up to the meeting, I prepared a report that covered the history of communes back to the Middle Ages and discussed the new American experiments.

When the discussion began, everyone seemed enthused about the idea. But there was no clear plan of how to go about it nor of how the commune would be organized in the first place. We had to find answers. It was self-evident that it had to be a political commune, a place where people could develop and practice a new way to do politics and to change society.

After the first meeting everyone wanted to meet again to continue the discussion. At the second meeting more people came, people I didn't know, as well as the ones I'd invited the first time. There was a man named Andreas and his wife, Helga. Andreas was an architect and he was inspired to design a house specifically as a commune where around sixty people could live. That was about how many people there were in our commune discussion group.

Not long after that, I got sick. While I was laying in bed, feeling a little feverish and weak, Rudi came in and said, "There are visitors for you."

"For me?" I said in surprise. Visitors were almost always for Rudi.

"Do you feel well enough to talk to them?"

"Yes," I said. Helga and Andreas came into the room and sat at the end of the bed, making themselves comfortable, trying to relax. I suspect they were a little amazed at their own chutzpah, daring to even come and afraid it wouldn't work out. I was surprised, since I'd only seen them a couple times at the commune group. I wasn't even sure of their names, but they introduced themselves again. We talked a little about where we came from. They could tell I was American from my accent. "Why did you come to Germany? Did you meet Rudi here or in the USA?"

"I was really aiming to study philosophy," I said. "But then I met Rudi here in Berlin. It changed everything."

They laughed.

"Are both of you from Berlin?" I asked.

Andreas said he was, but Helga originally came from West Germany. Andreas' family was an old Berlin family. Both of them were well-established families with money, educated-bourgeoisie is what the Germans call them, families whose prestige comes from education, and positions in cultural and educational institutions rather than the economy. Their families had not opposed the Nazis and now, as then, they supported the status quo.

Helga was more perturbed about her family's background than Andreas. Her father had been a Nazi and she wanted to atone. I think she saw it that way. It was incomprehensible to her that her father could have thought that way. She also believed that there was a part of Germany, the GDR, that had broken with the National Socialist tradition completely whereas West Germany had not. This was an illusion, which Rudi who knew East Germany as Helga did not, could not agree with.

Andreas said, "I have some ideas about a commune house and I've started working on a model. I also have an idea about where it could be built. There's an empty lot near the Oskar Helene Heim U-Bahn station."

"How much do you think that would cost?" I asked.

"A lot," Andreas said, "but if we split it between sixty people it could be done."

I thought the idea was fantastic, maybe more revolutionary than some of the more abstruse organizing and theoretical ideas they were discussing in the SDS. "I think we need to have both common areas where we can do things together and also a place of our own to withdraw when we want to be alone," I said. "It shouldn't be like a big dormitory."

"I agree," Andreas said. "I have made some plans. Do you want to see them?"

"Oh yes," I said.

He had some drawings, which he explained, and we discussed how the commune could function in some of the ways we wanted. I told Andreas he should definitely present his plan at the next commune group meeting.

When they left, I was feeling very encouraged. I liked them. I liked their ideas about practical communal living and building our own place. It was the first time I'd really felt as if there were people with whom I could build lasting friendships in Berlin.

I would feel a little nudge of happiness when I saw Helga at the commune meetings and we would sit together—we soon became close friends. She was different to most of the SDS people I'd met so far. There seemed to be something more substantial about her, at least in her relation to me. Most of the other women seemed bound to their boyfriends or perhaps they thought that I was, so I found no direct access to these women. I don't know why that was. Perhaps being married as I was may have carried a different status and women didn't expect to have the same kind of relationship with a married woman as

they did with other less attached women. Helga, being married, didn't have that barrier.

Everyone admired Andreas' plan for a commune house. But when it came to talking about how to finance it, the discussion faltered. The amount of money needed seemed too huge to be obtainable. If everyone could work just a few extra hours each week, it would be possible, mathematically speaking. But practically people did not know how they could get a job like that. It was a quandary and we weren't finding solutions. Still, there was a lot of enthusiasm for the idea.

About that time Rudi said, "Dieter Kunzelmann wants to come to Berlin."

"Why?" I asked in astonishment. I thought Dieter was a Munich fixture and that's where he belonged.

"He heard about the commune discussion," Rudi said, "he has ideas about communes and wants to join our group."

"Oh no," I groaned. "He will ruin it."

"He's only one person," Rudi said. "How could he ruin it?"

"He will," I said. "Mark my words. It is the way he treats people. He will behave the way he did last Christmas, like a pasha, negative and nasty." That is when I had met him for the first time.

Rudi looked a little perturbed. "Yes," he said. "But he is a revolution-

ary, and he is committed, and we don't have many like that. We need him for the revolution."

"But what kind of a revolution is that?" I asked.

Rudi didn't know what to say.

"Tell him not to come," I said.

"I don't think I can do that," said Rudi. "He can go where he wants to."

Dieter came to Berlin and joined the commune group. The atmosphere changed at once. It became more aggressive, more intolerant, polarized. Whereas before, I had imagined that we could live with everyone in the group and be happy, I now saw that it would bring unpleasant conflicts. When I'd say this to Rudi, he seemed a little disturbed because I was unhappy, but he didn't see it as a big problem, and he didn't think he could do anything about it anyway, except to present the kind of commune he thought we should have, a focus point for the revolution where we could develop our theory and praxis.

In the commune group, Dieter tried to dominate the discussion. He, of course, had his own ideas, which apparently he'd been pondering for a few years: the goal of the commune is to destroy our bourgeois personalities. They must be replaced by a new kind of person with a revolutionary personality.

I listened to this with dismay. What the new person would be like wasn't so clear. If he meant something like himself, all I could see was terrorizing others and oppression of women and human relationships far darker than what I'd ever known. It was not liberation in my view. But he thought that once the bourgeois tarnish was removed, the pristine person would automatically appear and apparently along with it the potential for a new society.

I already knew how Dieter would go about destroying the bourgeois personality. He had enough audacity to believe that he had pretty much already destroyed his own, so he would be the guru leading the others into destruction; by putting people down, denigrating them, forcing people to behave in the way he thought they should, forcing women to have sex with him if he wanted them or breaking up relationships he didn't like. As far as I could see, it wasn't a destruction of the bourgeois personality—on the contrary, it was an elevation of the destructive forces of a capitalist society, disconnection instead of solidarity, meanness instead of comradeship, competition instead of connection.

For Rudi it gradually became clear that this was not his notion of a focus group in which everyone worked together toward a political goal, or social change in broad society. Someone started calling Dieter's methods psycho-terror. And that was apt. As a result of all of this discussion and dissension the commune as a way of organizing daily life became less and less important for Rudi. For me it was a defeat, although I didn't completely give up hope. As Dieter's notion of commune gained the upper hand in the group, Rudi developed his idea of a focus group, which did not necessarily require living together. He still participated in the discussions, but talked about his focus idea as a way for revolutionaries to organize in their political work.

Although it was only a minority that was attracted to Dieter's commune idea, Rudi had not been able to form an active group to pursue his own ideas and my hope for a big commune with all sixty people withered. In the meantime, Dieter and eight of his followers found an apartment and moved in. They called their enclave Kommune I. Their escapades got good media attention and Kommune I quickly became famous. What happened inside their four walls, I don't know for sure, except that the sex experiment didn't work very well, because most of the men wanted to sleep with the same women and vice versa, and the ones left out were not happy. But they did carry out some fantastic actions, the most famous one being the pudding attack against US vice president Hubert Humphrey.

When Humphrey came to Berlin for a state visit, the Kommune prepared a pudding with red dye which they were going to throw at him. They practiced in the woods. Apparently, they were discovered or denounced by someone who thought this was some kind of napalm or other dangerous chemical mixture. The whole commune was arrested and put in jail and the headlines in the next day described a murderous plan that had been thwarted. When it turned out the dangerous chemicals consisted of pudding and red dye, everyone on the left laughed. Soon after, Kommune II was formed, but there were not enough people in this group to pursue Andreas' Commune House idea and the commune group discussions were discontinued. But in the following months and years, communes and community living experiments sprang up all over West Berlin and beyond, practicing various forms and degrees of a communal ideal.

New developments took place in our discussions. Berlin in the fall of 1966 was beginning to curdle. The USA was escalating its war in Vietnam, which had its effects here as well. There was no doubt that the generation who had grown up after World War II was coming of age, and that we were angry. Our parents didn't understand it. West German parents had rebuilt their country and thought they were building a peaceful and prosperous nest for their children. So why were these children so restless? American parents had created the most powerful country in the world and there too a growing middle class had become wealthier.

But the children who had not known much hardship seemed not to appreciate it. That annoyed some parents. It looked like a clash between the generations. But it wasn't that. There were real problems that our generation was facing far beyond an intransigent family. There was a cold war in which both sides were armed to the teeth with weapons of

mass destruction. No one knew if the crazy governments would use them, but they knew that if they did, the world as we knew it would go tumbling down. The USA flexing its muscles did not care for the desires of nations and peoples for their own independence.

But the liberation struggles of these nations and peoples were gaining attention and sympathy. In Germany, the parents who'd rebuilt their nation refused to talk about why it had been destroyed in the first place. The German youth wanted to know. But parents did not want anyone to talk about concentration camps or even see films with pictures of what they were like. Such films were, in fact, forbidden to be shown in public, so children didn't ask their parents. They had to get their information elsewhere. And a war of ideologies was going on; Communism vs. Capitalism. Both sides were trying to win the minds of the youth or scare them into submission.

For us, there was more than enough to do. We produced flyers, typing them, printing them, typing whole books about anti-authoritarianism, so that everyone in the organizations could read them. I knew enough German to type and I could type fast.

Rudi had started a Third World study group of students from all over the planet who were studying in Berlin. I also belonged to this group and each of us was to report on the political movements in our countries. The USA was not a Third World country, of course, but it was important nonetheless, because the opposition movements in the USA, in "the belly of the beast," would connect and join the liberation movements in other countries. So my task was to find out about the various groups in the USA and report on them.

I discovered that there was a group of leftist Americans in Berlin who worked with US soldiers stationed in Berlin. This consisted mostly of going to bars where soldiers congregated to discuss the war with them. Many would be going to Vietnam at some point and most of them didn't want to, so they were open to talking to our dissidents. The group had connections to Scandinavia, so those who wanted to desert would be given instructions for the underground railway that would get them to safety in Sweden.

One of the first political actions I participated in with Rudi happened at night. We were plastering posters all over West Berlin that said "The Bonn government supports MURDER. Murder using Napalm, murder using poison gas, nuclear murder? America's aggression in Vietnam serves US corporate greed. The people of Asia, Africa and Latin America are struggling against hunger, death and alienation. The former slaves want to be human beings. Capitalists react by killing them and making big profits at the same time. For those peoples the only answer is REVOLUTION. Amis get out of Vietnam! Signed International Liberation Front."

It was done in black, white and red. "Murder" was spelled out in big red letters.

I was supposed to sit with another person and listen to the police radio to see if they'd discovered the posters. If they were discovered, we were to let the poster plasterers know, so they could avoid being arrested. But the police found them before they could be warned and some were arrested. Then the police spent the rest of the night looking for the posters and tearing them down. But they missed a few, and a couple house owners whose buildings had been plastered actually liked the posters and wouldn't let the police rip them off. It was in the newspaper the next day, even if it was almost a fiasco. Rudi had bought all the dailies that morning and we poured over them, pleased at the apparent success.

A few weeks after that, we demonstrated in front of the Amerika Haus. Everyone stood there with anti-war signs and nothing happened. Police came, but did nothing. Then someone threw an egg at the Amerika Haus. It made a little splat, which no one could hear, because a big noisy truck drove past at that moment, but the shouts and laughter from the demonstrators were loud enough. More eggs went splat until the building was spotted with small white and yellow drippy polka dots. Everyone was shouting and the police started arresting people.

Sometime later I got arrested for the first time. Rudi was arrested too. We had discovered that smashing eggs against public buildings was annoying people, but not getting us any sympathy. In one of many SDS discussions people decided to do something nice to win people over. Flyers were produced—no confrontations with the police! Everyone was supposed to bring wine and offer some to people on the street. The demonstration was taking place on the sidewalk among pedestrians, no posters or banners, but flyers were being passed out with poetry about policemen who ought to go home and have a nice fuck with their wives instead of banging students over the head with their batons.

It was a Sixties kind of demonstration, flower power. But apparently the police missed the point. I was carrying two bottles of wine and Rudi had a box and a megaphone. The box was to stand on, so he could see over the crowds. Rudi wasn't very tall and he needed the box to be seen. He did have a very penetrating voice, but on a busy street full of Christmas shoppers and lots of traffic, even he couldn't yell loud enough for many to hear him. That's why he had the megaphone. We were walking along together among the crowds and the demonstrators so it wasn't so obvious who was who, looking for a good place where Rudi could stand and start talking to the people.

I saw the police car first. It was an ordinary police car, but it was full of policemen, packed in like sardines. That was odd. I pinched Rudi's arm and said, "look!". The car parked right beside us and the policemen poured out. Within a few seconds they had surrounded Rudi and grabbed him. I wasn't sure what would happen. It was very obvious that they wanted only Rudi. They started dragging him to the car. I tried to grab Rudi and pull him away, but they swatted me away like a fly. I started banging with my fists on the back of a policeman who held Rudi. But I had the feeling it was hurting my fists more than the policeman, like pounding on a brick wall. They ignored me and pushed Rudi into the car. I watched with a sinking feeling as the doors closed and the car pulled away. I was alone.

Then I saw some people I knew and ran up to them. "They arrested Rudi," I yelled nervously. "There, they went there," I pointed in the direction where the car was disappearing in the traffic.

"They took him?" the students asked surprised. "Why? What did he do?"

"He didn't do anything. We were just walking along. He had the megaphone. They took that, too."

"Ummm," they said, unsure of what to do. "We should each go a different way."

"Uh oh," I said . "Look." This time it was not a police car, but a paddy wagon. It stopped and a policeman got out, stared at me and then pointed at me and shouted "It's her.". Once again, a horde of policemen poured out and grabbed me, and the others who were standing there, pushing us into the wagon. It drove off to the police station.

By the time we got there other paddy wagons were unloading people, young mostly, but some older people too, most carrying bundles with their Christmas purchases. The men were led off in one direction, the women in another. I was pushed into a cage along with about ten other women. The door clanked behind me.

"Well," said I. "What now?" Everyone was looking a little baffled. One woman was almost crying. "Why did they do this? I was just shopping. I ... Look," she said and held up a bag that said KaDeWe.

"They're arresting everybody," another woman said. "They don't care who is part of the rally and who isn't."

An older woman said, "This reminds me of the Nazis. That's what they did."

"Is it a demonstration?," asked the women with the KaDeWe bag. "What is it about?"

"Well, actually it's for the police, and against the war in Vietnam," I said.

"I wonder how long they will keep us here."

"Who knows," said another.

I suddenly realized I was still holding my bag with the two wine bottles. "Well," I said. "I've still got these. They were supposed to be for the demonstration. So they're for us now. Let's open them. Even if we don't have food, at least we have this."

The other women thought that was a great idea. If people were nervous and a little distraught, the task of getting the bottles open distracted them. In a few minutes we were passing them around and started laughing about the situation.

The first bottle was soon empty and the second was half empty. I had been there for maybe two hours. More women had been brought in and the cage was getting quite full. A policeman came to the door and shouted, "Is Frau Dutschke here?"

I waved my hand, "Come," he said.

I was surprised. No one had been let out of the cage up until then. I wondered why I was being given this unusual treatment. The policeman opened the door.

"Hey, your bottle," someone yelled.

"Keep it," said I. "Drink it up." I followed the policeman down a long snot-yellow painted hall. Why were bureaucratic places like this always painted such a disgusting color? The fluorescent lights added to the sickening appearance.

"So, Frau Dutschke," the policeman said. "Your husband is in a cell in another part of the building."

"Can I see him?" I asked.

"No, he is alone. He isn't with the others."

I frowned and muttered, "why?"

The policeman ignored me. "He will be staying there for a while."

"How long?"

"I don't know," he said. "He said he will faint if he doesn't get any food."

"Oh," I said. I knew that wasn't true. He had never fainted, although as far as I knew he'd never been without food long enough to be starving, but I didn't contradict him.

"You can get him some food," said the policeman.

I was astonished. "You are letting me out to go and get food?"

"Yes, just come back here when you have it."

I didn't have much money with me, so I had to go home to get some. I then went to the Edeka store across the street from where we lived. I thought that everyone would be hungry, not just Rudi, so I bought as many groceries as I could carry and went back to the police station.

"Well," the policeman said, staring at my two bags. He seemed to be laughing, but I couldn't tell if it was friendly.

"I've got food," I said and held the two big bags out to him.

At that the policeman burst into laughter. "Do you think he is going to stay here forever?"

"No," said I, taken aback. "I hope he comes out soon. But the food is for everyone."

"For everyone." The policeman stared at me somewhat amused. "Well, you can't do that."

"I can't do what?"

"You can't give food to everyone. Only to your husband."

I was a little annoyed. The bags were heavy, I'd schlepped them a long way and I knew people were getting hungry. "I want everyone to have this food. I can't take it back again. It's too heavy."

He shook his head. "It's against the rules,"

"Oooph," said I even more annoyed. "Well, maybe you can do it anyway." I pushed the two bags into his hands and if he hadn't taken them they would have fallen to the floor. He didn't say anything, so I turned to go.

"I'll give it to your husband," he said.

"He can't eat that much," I said. "Don't let it go to waste." I started walking away before he could change his mind about taking the food, or even about letting me go.

That evening, I went to bed without Rudi. I couldn't sleep, though. I wondered about the fainting thing. Maybe he did faint. Just because I'd never seen it, didn't mean it couldn't have happened. I worried about how long he'd be in jail and what would happen to him. All night I twisted and turned. It was already beginning to get a little light outside when I finally drifted off to sleep. But the sound of the key in the door woke me again. Rudi came in and crawled into bed beside me as quietly as he could.

"I'm not asleep," I murmured. "Are you OK?"

"I'm fine," he said and put his arm around me.

"I'm glad you're back," I said.

There were more rallies, many more. Most of them blended into a blur of masses of people in the streets holding signs saying Amis out of Vietnam, or Johnson baby killer, or red and blue Vietcong flags with a yellow star, of voices chanting, Ho Ho Ho Chi Minh, of policemen either standing by in threatening knots, holding shields, wearing Bismarckian helmets, wielding batons, or moving in to arrest people, grabbing them, dragging them to paddy wagons. Once when they grabbed me I started talking in English, so they let me go.

But it got worse for the protesters. The attacks by the police became more violent and finally deadly. Indeed, it was a revolution full of contradictions, sometimes violent, but it changed the country, in the end for the better. It turned an authoritarian tradition of obedience to a new culture of anti-authoritarian public discourse on the meaning of democracy and set off a democratization of social institutions in Germany.

Now, more than fifty years later it is still providing a barrier against the world-wide spread of the culture of hate. But that barrier may not be impenetrable. It is time to revive the struggle for a culture of solidarity with our fellow human beings and with our endangered environment.

Gretchen Dutschke was born in Illinois in 1942. After her bachelor in 1963, she studied theology in Germany. There she met Rudi Dutschke; they married in 1966 and have three children. In 1985, five years after Rudi's death, she went to the U.S., but returned to Berlin in 1990. She has written a biography about her husband and has also published the book 1968: What We Can Be Proud Of. *Photo: private*

Pretty Sigi and the Skyscraper

By Paul F. Duwe

WHEN YOU SPIN a top, it begins to hum. In this regard, the name "Kreisel," which is the German word for "top," suited a construction project just fine, because a few people put quite a bit of no good into motion with it. Though, oddly enough, no one actually had to "hum," or rather, go to jail. But when there's talk in West Berlin of the "mother of all scandals," it comes pretty close to the reality of the three-sector city inside the wall. The Steglitzer Kreisel, that thirty-story skyscraper at the end of the shopping mile on Schlossstrasse, right by a traffic hub and visible from far and wide and under construction for twelve long years, from 1968 to 1980, became a symbol of megalomania and blind faith in the future for West German society.

After the Second World War, Berlin was an abused, rubble-filled wasteland, and hundreds of thousands of Berliners had fled to West Germany. Soon, however, the surviving generation got right down to work, gazing steadily at the future. An assertive drive coupled with a healthy dose of impertinence—just like the clocks have always ticked in Berlin.

West Berlin was firmly under Social Democratic control at the time: many of the city's top brass were dyed-in-the-wool Social Democrats who wanted to rebuild the free part of the city. They were also anti-communists—in defiance of the Soviets who controlled the Eastern part. Among the top brass, there was major Willy Brandt, who would later become chancellor of Germany, and his successor Klaus Schütz, along with Building Senator Rolf Schwedler and Finance Senator Heinz Striek.

Once the rubble was cleared, things could really start rolling. High, higher, highest. Skyscrapers were a must. A golden age for new greatness. That's what many thought during the economic wonder years of the 1950s, which would by no means pass by the west sectors in Berlin. In the showcase of the "free world," subsidies sparkled early and far more luxuriantly than anything else. A general Berlin allowance for everybody ramped up salaries, sports clubs received travel allowances for trips to West Germany. And school classes from Heilbronn to Wilhelmshaven took a publicly financially supported stroll along the Kurfürstendamm.

But that wasn't enough. When the Wall was built on August 13, 1961, the situation intensified dramatically. Now it was a matter of West Berlin's very survival. The Cold War defined not only politics, but everyday life as well. In this serious situation, the western sectors and their approximately two million inhabitants were in urgent need of support. And so, the federal government in Bonn passed the Berlin Aid Act in 1964. The idea was to promote financial investments in West Berlin, especially giant construction projects, with tax incentives. Well intentioned, but it turned the island into a hotbed of write-off artists of all kinds.

This is when the story of the pretty, ambitious Sigrid Kressmann-Zschach and the Steglitzer Kreisel begins. The architect built a residential building in the early 1960s on Hermann-Ehlers-Plaz, near the Steglitz city hall. There she discovered in passing that a large subway stop was to be developed beneath the neighboring, still downright rundown property. That meant the area above the subway stop would also be developed. It was a unique opportunity for an architect whose motto was, "you can never have enough men, houses, or money."

Many interesting ideas for using the plot of land were debated, including a new home for the district's city hall on nearby Schlossstrasse, which was much too small. At first the new city hall was to be a modest building. But the Senate's construction department, which overrode the district, had completely different plans. There was talk of "urban building dominance." This approach pleased Sigrid Kressmann-Zschach, and she quickly changed her game plan.

First the property issue had to be resolved, because the area consisted of several plots held by different owners. The SPD-led senate and Mayor Willy Brandt initially wanted to motivate a labor union association to purchase the land. A number of important public functions were planned for the area, after all, including the subway station and a bus terminal.

What happened next was like the race between the tortoise and the hare. The clever Kressmann-Zschach set to work acquiring parcels of land, while union enterprises in Hamburg were valiantly bargaining with the senate's construction department. At one point, a delegate from the Hanseatic City arrived at Tempelhof Airport and was met, to his surprise, by his competitor. Kressmann-Zschach had simply been faster. In early 1967, she procured the key plot of land, Albrechtstrasse 1a, and the Hamburg contingent was no longer in the running. In the Schlossstrasse game of Monopoly, there was one clear winner.

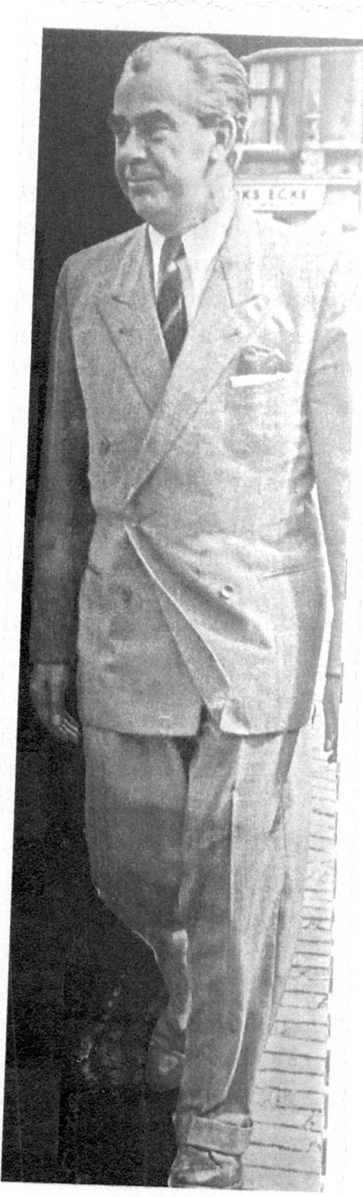

How did an architect's daughter born in Leipzig in 1929 manage to pull off a real-estate coup like that? Sigrid Kressmann-Zschach was a phenomenon of Berlin society. With her classy appearance, the architect drew the attention of everyone around her. "She was a very attractive and beautiful woman," her contemporaries recalled years later, with utmost respect. She arrived in Berlin in the 1950s and married Willy "Texas-Willy" Kressmann a few years later. Kressmann was a local politician who was known throughout the city. The leftwing Social Democrat, born in Prenzlauer Berg, had fled the Nazis and was eventually detained in England. In 1949, Kressmann—depicted on the right in a life-size picture at the Willy-Kressmann-Stadion for soccer in Kreuzberg—became mayor of the borough of Kreuzberg.

Toward the end of the fifties, Kressmann undertook a state visit in Texas and became an honorary citizen of San Antonio. He acquired a white cowboy hat, which he wore in Berlin a lot. This led to his nickname, "Texas-Willy." He also was impressed with the freedom he had experienced in the America.

This was not the end of Kressmann's relationship with the United States. In 1962, the Socialist went to the USA on a speaking tour. After an appearance in New York City on June 5, he made it onto the front page of *The New York Times*. At a press conference, he urged then-President Dwight D. Eisenhower to resume the Four-Power-Talks with the Soviet Union, Great Britain, and France. This would be necessary to prevent a Third World War and to pace the way to an undivided Europe, he said. He also asked for economic help for East Germany, because the Soviets were not the only ones responsible for the Berlin Wall; the Western powers were also to blame. The Wall was a "result of the politics of the East and the West." This was, mind you, ten months after the Wall was built. This caused quite a scandal at home (and was not well received in America, either).

The head of the "Free Republic of Kreuzberg," or, of "Kressmannsdorf," as the borough was occasionally nicknamed, naturally had the best contacts in the divided city's political establishment, where the SPD still had absolute rule. Those contacts opened doors for his young wife, which likely would have remained closed to her without her prominent husband. And Sigrid Kressmann-Zschach, called "SKZ" for short, was quite comfortable in the West Berlin biotope. She quickly took advantage of the opportunity to apply the right spin to her own interests.

Her marriage to "Texas-Willy" was over by 1962, after only two years. Perhaps the glamorous architect and the down-to-earth Socialist weren't such a good match after all. But the foundation for the advancement of "Pretty Sigi" had been laid. There was no stopping SKZ. She established an ambitious construction company, which soon topped three hundred employees. In the man's world of the German real-estate game, she ascended with charm and skill to become an icon of architecture. The press acknowledged her as "an unusually clever businesswoman."

In January 1968, the bustling building tycoon had added the key parcel at the planned subway station to her portfolio. In addition, the urban freeway ended there, which forced the Senate to contact the fledgling property owner, whether it wanted to or not. Leading Senate officials always doubted that this constellation came about coincidentally, suspecting a "guiding hand" at the highest level. But who that might have been was never revealed.

Whatever the circumstances, Kressmann-Zschach really got down to business. The Kreisel project would become the capstone of her hitherto brilliant career. She established a company for the project, by the name of Avalon. The business objective of this limited company and limited partnership was originally listed as industrial laundry. But soon the company, known by employees as the "Island of the Holy," concentrated solely on the planned Kreisel.

For her project, Pretty Sigi needed a partner with money. She found one in the respected Swiss financier Jacques Rosenstein. With him, the Senate erroneously believed, the skyscraper project was off to a good start. In summer 1969, the Berlin House of Representatives voted in favor of the largest private construction project to date in the western part of the city. The budget was valued at around one hundred eighty million marks, which would be a little less than four hundred million dollars today. This looked to everyone involved like a realistic amount, though it already represented a dramatic cost increase. Just one year earlier, they had been talking about only eighty million marks.

Financier Rosenstein was to collect the requisite limited-partner capital from two Frankfurt institutions. Yet despite the ample opportunities for write-offs, the money wasn't flowing in the amounts anticipated. When the Senate required an additional personal liability from Rosenstein, he threw in the towel. The Tower of Steglitz was approaching the make-or-break point, though this would not become clear to those politically responsible until much later. For Kressmann-Zschach, however, the project continued without Rosenstein for the time being. She took on his shares and held all the reins. Which meant there was no internal inspection. Finance Senator Heinz Striek (SPD) said later, "It was an unholy union, having the construction chief and architect in one person."

But in the early phase of construction, the Avalon boss allowed no room for doubt. On May 14, 1969, the first pile was driven. For ten floors, there was a firm rental commitment from the Steglitz district City Hall. Steglitz was nearing a population of 190,000, a big city within a metropolis. Naturally, the city's investment was to be taken seriously. And money did not play much of a role anyway. SKZ went right on building.

In September 1972, a downright ostentatious topping-out ceremony was held, and there was no stopping the euphoria of the West Berlin Social Democratic VIPs. Klaus Schütz, governing mayor of Berlin at the time, gushed, "A big idea that will prove itself." Though increasingly critical voices were growing louder, Schütz dismissed them with strong

words: "These premature judgments are nothing more than bitter, envious, and uncalled-for grumbling."

And yet, the mayor probably should have noticed that the total costs had risen another one hundred twenty million in just three years, to three hundred million marks. But more than a hundred million marks in direct or guaranteed national funds had already been sunk into the project. Now money was getting tight; only one year after the topping-out ceremony, the first funding shortfall of at least ten million marks became apparent. Others would follow. With that, the largest Berlin construction scandal since the end of the war had run its course.

For the Berlin city government, it became all about rescuing the vanity project. Not only the Senate's reputation was on the line—the West German taxpayer had also sunk a lot of money into the high-rise. Then, on top of that, at the end of 1974, the limited partners' tax incentive ended. But the tower had to be finished. Or else the entire, politically well-established system of Berlin subsidies would become discredited.

Only Sigrid Kressmann-Zschach did not let this malaise get her down, preferring to feather her own nest. She knew exceedingly well how to "sling the public purse around her slender waist," Günter Matthes, the influencal metro editor of the Berliner *Tagesspiegel*, wrote in his column, "Am Rande bemerkt" (Marginal Notes). The honorarium of the star architect, who had a villa in Halensee and a penthouse apartment in Schöneberg, was about forty million marks.

Unfortunately, all attempts to pull the cart out of the mud ended up the same. The limited partners were not able to remargin on short notice the thirty million marks required at the time. Nor did the Senate want to throw good money at the bad. On April 25, 1974, Avalon entered bankruptcy. In the weeks leading up to that point, the police had closely guarded the construction site, to prevent looting.

As early as fall 1973, a fact-finding commission in the House of Representatives had formed. It had also carefully scrutinized the KuDamm-Karree, another Kressmann-Zschach building on financially weak footing. The commission was to review a "potential alliance between private and public interests." This seemed completely reasonable, because in addition to the murky business practices of Avalon, other scandals had occurred, which had long been the talk of the town.

Alone among men, Sigrid Kressmann-Zschach masterfully brought other weapons to bear. Finance Senator Striek had a deputy, a Senate director by the name of Klaus Arlt, who had gotten very close to SKZ personally. The two met every now and then at the Pension Zur Tanne in the Harz Mountain town of Braunlage, for example, where they shared a room, but also in Vienna's fancy Hotel Sacher.

For the Berlin press, the Sachertorte encounters were naturally great fodder. There was speculation that they spent time there not solely for extremely personal matters but also for business. Even if the affair played no verifiable role in the Kreisel project, that kind of interaction between a builder and a Senate director was a source of public consternation. Arlt, off whose shoulders the criticism apparently rolled completely, stated before the fact-finding commission that SKZ was a clever architect who "had a rather tough time as a woman."

Without the shimmering character of Sigrid Kressmann-Zschach, the Kreisel-scandal probably would have failed in a less spectacular way. She knew how to beguile her conversation partners in such a manner that some men would feel as if they'd faint. Particularly because her technical expertise was indisputable. *Süddeutsche Zeitung* once wrote that Kressmann-Zschach had become the "cleverest female builder on the European continent." The outcome of the Kreisel adventure proved that assessment wrong. The architect had built too much on sand.

For some time, the Senate actually considered demolishing the unfinished construction. But work began on it again in 1977, after a Berlin entrepreneur had bought the property at auction. In 1980, the first tenants were able to move in: the Steglitz City Hall, and some offices of the state of Berlin, which rented not only ten floors, but nearly the entire Kreisel. Construction costs were about four times the first estimates from 1968. Still, the Steglitz high-rise was at least completed.

But it would become a symbol for one particular specialty of the half-city, West Berlin corruption. That non-transparent combination of personal ambition and political and economic lobbying, parties, organizations, companies, and institutions would pull the subsidized metropolis into the spotlight many more times in the 1980s.

The perfect disaster did not remain without political consequences. In a vote in the Berlin House of Representatives on March 2, 1975, the Christian Democrats became the strongest party in West Berlin for the first time since it was founded after World War II. While the SPD was at first able to form a coalition with the Liberals and continue ruling, its image was considerably damaged. In April 1975, Striek stepped down, the most prominent victim of the affair; Arlt was suspended. One year later, Schwedler also left politics. Klaus Schütz continued serving as governing mayor until 1977, when he also stepped down.

When the Kreisel was opened, not only SKZ had fallen from grace, but her former husband Texas Willy had experiences a falling out with the SPD as well. His 1962 remarks in New York City about the mutual responsibility for the Wall in the East and in the West had put him under intense pressure in Berlin and especially from the incensed comrades.

Soonafter, he left not just the party, but Berlin altogether. He moved to the tiny village of Rottach-Egern in the Bavarian Alps, the most southern part of Germany, and did not return to Kreuzberg until a few months before his death in 1986. Four years later, in October 1990, Sigi, his ex-wife, died of cancer. She was only sixty-one years old.

Around that time, just ten years after its dedication, the Steglitzer Kreisel made the headlines again. This time it was because asbestos was found in the building. The fight over the cost and the manner of remediation was also a lengthy one. The Kreisel was evacuated in 2007, due to the dangerous substance. The high rise stood empty for a long time—also at considerable financial damage to the state of Berlin.

Only after removal of the asbestos did a new chapter begin for the hapless landmark on Schlossstrasse. A large building contractor took over the Kreisel in 2017. The plan was to fill the high rise with condominiums—more than three hundred. However, those plans fell apart as well. The building was sold, and resold, and resold again—currently, it is still empty and in construction; or rather, it would be in construction, had those not been halted by a variety of lawsuits.

Will the Kreisel ever become a place to live and work again? The view from the three hundred-fifty feet tower over Berlin would surely be breathtaking. Almost as breathtaking as Sigi Kressmann-Zschach.

Paul F. Duwe, born in 1953 in the GDR, grew up in Mecklenburg. He left the country in 1971 for West Germany after his father, a political prisoner, was released. He studied journalism at Free University in West Berlin and worked as a Metro reporter for Spandauer Volksblatt. *Since 1986, he has been a freelance journalist. His first novel* Petermännken *was published in 2008.* *Photo: René Worlitzer*

SCHUHE
gefallen immer
BERLIN
FRANKFURT
HAMBURG
ARKADAŞ KEBAB
SALONU
EIS
DÖNER KEBAP

From Wedding to Wilmersdorf

By Erkan Arikan

I WAS BORN in Turkey, in a small harbor town on the Sea of Marmara in 1969, as my parents' first child. In fact, my life should have played out in West Turkey, where my father was employed as an accountant for a German–Turkish farming operation. Maybe I would have followed in my father's footsteps. But everything, and I do mean everything, turned out quite differently.

When I arrived with my mother at the Berlin-Tempelhof airport on April 18, 1970, at the age of fourteen months, I did not know that this city would forever shape me and long be my home. My father had arrived in Berlin six months before we did, a classic guest worker of the first generation. He found an apartment in the borough of Wedding, which was common then for Turkish immigrants. The apartment was at Graunstrasse 14, on the edge of Prenzlauer Berg, near what is now the Mauerpark. It was cheap. The old West Berliners did not want to live so close to the Wall back then, which is why you rarely saw any German workers in Wedding.

I could barely walk when my path took me to the nursery school just one hundred fifty feet from our apartment. I spent the first four years of my life there and in the apartment. There were six renters in our building: two of them were other families of Turkish heritage, one of them was the bachelor Mr. Rudolph, who washed his Mercedes in the courtyard every Sunday, and two were known to us as "Auntie Schulz" and "Uncle Erwin." I didn't know Auntie Schulz's real name, but for the sake of being polite, that's what my parents wanted me to call this neighbor, a woman about sixty years old. And so I often spent time with Auntie Schulz and Uncle Erwin. When I rang their doorbell, Auntie Schulz, always wearing an apron, would open the door and say, "Well, Little Erki, here to watch the telly?"

But it wasn't about watching television. The couple had a sizable collection of tin soldiers in a large display case, which Uncle Erwin had obtained throughout the course of his life. We played with them together. Uncle Erwin was my pal and somehow also my uncle.

At first, I thought Uncle Erwin was my father's brother, because he greeted my father in the corridor with the words, "Good morning, Brother, we go shopping, you needing cigar?" Uncle Erwin smoked cigars, but for some reason, he never smoked in my presence.

And so I lived on Graunstrasse in Wedding. The housing community was great, just like my nursery school. I still remember Auntie Christa, who was actually named Mrs. Altmann and was the school director, and my friends André Theiler and Arzu.

It was a terrific time. I could already speak German well, or rather “Berlinerisch.” Auntie Schulz and Uncle Erwin were the first ones I could just about communicate with by the age of three. As I could already speak so much then, Auntie Christa pulled me aside before lunch shortly before Christmas. I was to recite a poem for our Christmas assembly. I was able to memorize it quickly. And because we lived in Wedding, I recited the poem by Eduard Möricke like a true Berliner—pronouncing all the Gs like Y-sounding Js and the CHs like SHs.

Die heilije Nacht

Jesegnet sei die heilije Nacht,
die uns das Lischt der Welt jebracht! -
Wohl unterm lieben Himmelszelt
die Hirten lagen auf dem Feld.

Ein Engel Gottes, lischt und klar,
mit seinem Jruß tritt auf sie dar.
Vor Angst sie decken ihr Angesischt,
da sprischt der Engel: “Fürcht’ eusch nischt!“

Isch verkünd euch jroße Freud:
Der Heiland ist jeboren heut.
Da jehn die Hirten hin in Eil,
zu schaun mit Augen ditt ewije Heil;

zu singen dem süßen Jast Willkomm,
zu bringen ihm ein Lämmschen fromm.
Bald kommen auch gezogen fern
die heilgen drei König’ mit ihrem Stern.

Sie knieen vor dem Kindlein hold,
schenken ihm Myrrhen, Weihrauch, Jold.
Vom Himmel hoch der Engel Heer
frohlocket: “Jott in der Höh sei Ehr!“

This would be my last Christmas performance at the nursery school. It wasn’t until many, many years later that I returned to my nursery school. This time it was with my own children. Honestly, I had tears in my eyes. Everything was almost exactly as it was in 1974. Only the playground had been updated—with a modern adventure playground equipment. But I didn't dare go inside. I wanted my nursery school to stay in my memory just as it was when I left it forty-five years before.

Wedding was something special. We lived not far from Humboldthain—a large park that had a swimming pool. I went to the park almost every day with my nursery school class—along the former AEG building and the perfumery on Brunnenstrasse, owned by Bubi Scholz, the famous Berlin boxer. As a small child, I thought that was the whole of Berlin. But soon I learned that it was only West Berlin or, more precisely, only a part of it. It was an enclave from which we guest workers could flee to East-Berlin from time to time. My father once took me with him to the Friedrichstrasse train station. To me, it was thrilling, but as a nearly four-year-old, I obviously did not understand what it meant to live in a divided city.

We played outside on the street all day and only had to go home when it got dark. "Erkan, oğlum eve gel!" my mother called from the balcony of our apartment on the second floor, which meant something like, "Erkan, my son, come home." But I didn't know then that my days in that terrific district were already numbered.

Our building on Graunstrasse was slated to be torn down. Why? What for? Where to? All questions I didn't know the answers to at the age of four, nor did I want to. Right where our building was, the housing agency wanted to put up a senior residence. Instead of staying there in my own four walls with our beloved vaulted ceilings, in the Kiez, where I already knew every corner by the age of four, we had to leave.

The housing agency offered us a new apartment in a whole other part of Berlin. And so, I moved from one "W" to another—from Wedding to Wilmersdorf! This was a borough we guest-worker kids only heard in connection with the singular C & A department store back then on Ku'Damm. My parents were always convinced that C & A was in Wilmersdorf. No idea why. Much later, I learned that the fashion store was really in Charlottenburg. Maybe it was because we lived a mere stone's throw from the borough's edge.

I took my leave from Mr. Rudolph in our building, and from Auntie Schulz and Uncle Erwin. "You'll visit us, little guy, right?" were the last words she said to me, in tears. " 'Course I will!'" But I never did. Auntie

Schulz died just a few months after we moved away. I never saw Uncle Erwin again, either.

When we arrived in our new apartment in Wilmersdorf, it was right before Christmas again. It snowed so much that the gorgeous snow stayed on the streets and sidewalks for a long time. Our new home was—

and still is today—in the well cared-for so-called Bavarian Quarter, on Geisbergstrasse, not far from the famous KaDeWe department store on Wittenbergplatz. I noticed two things right away: first, the buildings were simpler and not plastered, with hardly any old buildings, and second, I didn't hear any Turkish, Arabic, Spanish, Yugoslavian, or Greek on the streets. Only German.

My parents spoke German themselves. But only when absolutely necessary, just what a man and woman working in a Siemens factory needed for their daily work. That was to be different for me. My parents wanted me to speak Turkish with them at home, but otherwise, I was to speak German. Of course, that's what I did. And I also established contacts in our building, like I had in Wedding. Housing Community was writ large, in our family. We quickly got to know the neighbors from across the hall, Mr. and Mrs. Koch, a couple the same age as my grandparents, and Mrs. Krüger on the ground floor. I would be bound to her in a friendship lasting over thirty years, until her death a few years ago. The Gorges family lived on the second floor. Their son Christian would become like a brother to me, and his parents, Lore and Dieter, like my second parents. And Mrs. Vieck from the first floor would become "Granny Helga" for my two daughters, many decades later.

My parents wanted me to demonstrate in my daily life the politeness and friendliness they had taught me. Of course I greeted every neighbor with a "Yoo'day" or "Yood ev'nin.'," so, Berlin slang for "good day" and good evening". But everything was different in Wilmersdorf. It took a long time for a community to develop in our building. Our Turkish friends frequently came to visit us on weekends. And when Turks came to visit, they did not stay for a few hours, but for half the night. So, sometimes the noise level in the keen-eared building was a bit louder.

Once my parents found an anonymous note in their mailbox. "Dear Family Arikan, we would be very grateful if your friends would leave the building quietly and in a civilized manner, in keeping with renters' conventions!" My parents had only one motto: Don't attract attention or cause problems. From that day forward, our friends went down the four flights in their stockings only. My father never asked who might have written the note. That didn't matter at all.

Soon afterward, I went to school in Wilmersdorf—by myself, and in the afternoon I walked home alone from the after-school center. I was what we called a latchkey kid in those days. But we remained the only Turks on our street. When I had just turned six, I had a formative conversation with a married couple I knew from grocery shopping. In hindsight, I think the couple never knew that I was a Turk, because no one could tell by my accent. At some point the pair asked me if the woman with the headscarf, who regularly came to our house with the shopping basket, was our cleaning woman. No, that isn't our cleaning woman, that's my mother. The couple was shocked. I don't know why. Maybe because they were ashamed, because they made assumptions based on clichés and prejudice.

When I turned seven and moved up to the second grade, my sister was born. Shortly before, my father also got his driver's license, which is why we drove to Turkey in a car for the first time that summer. My father's first car was a VW K70. A yellow car with a black plastic roof. More than just a visual statement, that car would result in a formative experience for my father with the division of criminal investigation. But more on that later.

As soon as I had my grades in hand, I had to hurry home from school, because we wanted to leave right on grade day. My parents came straight home from work; the suitcases had been packed a few days earlier. We not only took clothes, but also two suitcases full of presents and a color TV for my uncle. Fully laden, we drove in the late afternoon over the Hohenzollerndamm and then took the autobahn entrance of the city ring road toward the border crossing point at Dreilinden.

Via the Avus autobahn, we arrived in Dreilinden in about half an hour, where we had to wait in traffic for more than four hours in the hot sun. After crossing the West Berlin border, we rolled into the East. We watched our passports travel via conveyor belt to the border control agent. "Goin' back to the homeland, eh?" the border control agent asked my father. "No, home Wilmersdorf! Visit family in Turkey!" my father answered. I don't think the agent really understood him, but as I would learn from a Turkish saying later, "Home is not where you're born, but where you are full."

The drive along the transit route is forever etched in my memory. "Baboom—pause—baboom—pause—baboom!" That's how it sounded to me as our car drove over the concrete slabs of the autobahn.

My father focused on the traffic, my mother sat in back with my sister, who was still a baby, and I sat in front with my father. No one banished me to the back seat, because it was normal back then for kids to sit in front. Because my father was a heavy smoker, I also learned early on that a seven-year-old should never inhale while lighting an "Ernte 23" cigarette. The first time, I felt like I'd been shot to another planet. That was not the last cigarette I lit for my father. Many would follow on the drive down and on the return trip as well.

After vacationing in Turkey for five weeks, we were all anxious about driving back to Berlin, again along the transit route through East Germany. Over two thousand miles later, we passed through Dreilinden once more. When we saw the statue of the Berlin bear on the autobahn, it was clear: We were home! But my father wanted to sell our VW K70 again in fall 1976. I didn't know why, because my mother and I liked the car. My father took me along to the private car mart on Beusselstrasse and presented the car. My father and a man at the mart soon came to an agreement, and the yellow VW K70 with the black plastic top changed hands.

Weeks later, my father received a letter from the police, stating that he had not paid citations all over Germany. Back then, just like now, no one wanted any stress with the authorities, so my father took a day off from work to go to the registration office on Rudolstädter Strasse. There he learned that the man who bought the car had not transferred the registration, not even over three months later. My father showed the purchase agreement, the buyer's ID number, and the letter from the insurance company, stating that the car was no longer in his possession, to the clerk on the fourth floor of the building.

As it turned out, the buyer's ID number was stolen. And not only that, the stolen ID number was associated with a man the police suspected of with ties to the RAFs, the terrorist organization which had Germany on edge at the time. Unfortunately, my father had to pay the fines himself. My parents never found out who the buyer with the stolen ID number was. That would be the first and last time my father had any contact with the police. Since 1976, my father has not been cited for even so much as a parking ticket.

In conclusion, I would like to share my best and at the same time most embarrassing experience. Around the corner from our apartment in Wilmersdorf, on the corner of Lietzenburger and Nürnberger Streets, there was a Berlin cabaret theater, the "Wühlmäuse." Dieter Hallervorden, a founder of the cabaret and a local Berlin celebrity, often parked his car on Geisbergstrasse. My parents and I were big fans of his TV show, *Nonstop Nonsense* with Dieter Hallervorden, which aired on the ARD channel back then. Once in a while, "Didi" shopped at Bolle, the long-defunct supermarket associated with the C. Bolle Dairy Farm.

Because my mother also often shopped at Bolle, it was bound to occur that we would run into Didi there at some point. As a child, I was rather shy and very quickly embarrassed. But not my mother. We saw Dieter Hallervorden running across the street, and what did my mother do? She called, “Hello, Didi, I love you!” Everyone passing by turned around and started laughing.

I stood there wishing the ground would swallow me up. But not my mother. For her, the declaration of “I love you” was something normal, because in Turkish, you say, “Seni seviyorum,” which is harmless. Because my mother was also waving, the whole thing was even more embarrassing. I tried to move away from her, but as an eight-year-old boy, I wasn’t strong enough. What I didn’t expect, however, was that Dieter Hallervorden would laugh with a wave and “I love you, too!” and make everyone on Geisbergstrasse laugh. Including me.

Erkan Arikan grew up in Berlin and studied law at Free University. From 1999 to 2003, he worked for the news channel n-tv, where he had also done his traineeship. From 2003 to 2018, he headed the Turkish editorial department of the public broadcaster WDR. In November 2018, he was hired by Deutsche Welle, where he became head of the Turkish editorial department. *Photo: DW / B. Scheid*

ALLIED CHECKPOINT
US ARMY CHECKPOINT

The Trek of the Draft Resisters

Von Ulli Kulke

In spring 1970, Bernd Schaper's landlady pushed a letter through the slot in the door of his student apartment in Berlin-Zehlendorf. It looked like it might have been sent by his grandmother or Uncle Herbert. The address in elegant handwriting, blue ink on a green envelope, with Federal President Gustav Heinemann on the stamp. The scribbled sender: Matthias Reske from Braunschweig.

Bernd Schaper was from Braunschweig but he did not know anyone by the name of Matthias Reske. He opened the letter anyway, with a growing sense of what it might be about. He was right. This unknown Mr. Reske was informing him of something. Though not on official letterhead, it was a summons to report for his army physical in three weeks. At the district recruiting office at Grünewaldstrasse 12 in Braunschweig, in accordance with § 17.3 of the Compulsory Military Service Act. Schaper swore softly and put the letter back in the envelope.

The same letter had arrived at the home of Schaper's erstwhile classmate Ulf Merten, who was also a student at the Free University. Both were living in West Berlin, where there was no compulsory service—which is precisely why they had moved there. But the letter made the two a little uneasy. Would they really pass undetected? They also had planned to visit their hometown at Christmas. Would someone from the military police be waiting for them at the border crossing point in Helmstedt, at the end of the transit route, once they entered the Federal Republic, with its compulsory military service? No way to know, but best not to answer this strange letter.

Bernd and Ulf were not the only ones. They were part of a big wave of young men who had set off for West Berlin to avoid compulsory service. They were known around the country as Drückeberger— draft dodgers. Men who were not inclined to fulfill their obligatory military or civil service. There were tens of thousands of them from 1955, when compulsory military service was re-introduced under Konrad Adenauer, until the fall of the Wall. Maybe even hundreds of thousands. *Der Spiegel* wrote shortly after the fall of the Wall that ten thousand men had taken off for West Berlin, year after year.

Berlin was their goal, because its Four-Powers status did not allow compulsory military service in the city. And not only that, the Allies also prohibited West Berlin authorities from apprehending military refugees from West Germany. The exact number was never known. Many went even further. Former Federal Defense Minister Kai-Uwe von Hassel, a Christian Democrat, complained at a party defense policy meeting in 1964 that more than thirty thousand military refugees annually dodged service in the Federal Armed Forces, through cunning and trickery.

Their motivations varied widely, from personal aversion to opposition to everything military. Wolfgang from Hildesheim was a typical case. Wolfgang had fallen in love six months ago and now felt as if it would kill him to go for months without his daily tête-à-tête with his girlfriend during his basic military service. Yet even alternative civilian service usually meant living in the barracks, far from home. Not falling asleep in bed next to his sweet girl, but instead in a cot next to smelly, snoring men—if at all possible—no thank you!

Because his reasons would not likely sway any commission, Wolfgang claimed political grounds. He wasn't the only one; many young men like him honestly simply couldn't be bothered. Others didn't try any tricks but confessed their "total refusal" outright, despite the fact that the Compulsory Military Service Act afforded severe consequences, even prison time. Total refusniks considered military and civil service alike to be instruments of the "war machine." There are no credible estimates of how many young men escaped life in the barracks over the decades, or at least tried to. Besides the few openly total refusniks, most were more inclined to carry out their personal refusal on the quiet.

Helmut from Hamburg, for example, was one of them. Helmut was raised in the home of a church family; his father was a superintendent, and his mother a theologian. The family was united in its pacifism, so the military armed forces were out of the question. Many an evening meal saw the family wondering where Helmut would be summoned for alternative civilian service, but Helmut found the hullaballoo of the refusnik scene abhorrent; he wanted to get to West Berlin as soon as possible. He had friends there, who were active in the KPD/ML, the Communist Party of Germany/Marxist-Leninists, and he wanted to join them. He had not time for either armed military service or alternative civil service.

For some of these boys, their dread of the armed forces was so great that even West Berlin was not far enough. They chose life in the GDR instead and disappeared there. No one really knows how many there

were, but it might have been hundreds. Such a decision was usually hastily made: Most of them, according to Ulrich Bröckling in his book, *Armeen und ihre Deserteure* (Armies and their Deserters), subsequently were frustrated. They returned—via emigration application or the adventure of escaping from the GDR— to the West, "where they could expect not only punishment for desertion but also for traitorous relations."

Avoiding military service was no trivial offense. Paragraph 109 of the Criminal Code, Compulsory Service Refusal by Means of Mutilation, or 109a, Compulsory Service Refusal by Means of Deceit, established prison terms up to five years in length. In practice, most punishments were shorter and suspended. As a result, those affected might have taken the words of Minister von Hassel on successful service dodgers almost as an encouragement. He called them "clever boys" at the aforementioned CDU conference.

In any case, the intellectuals—von Hassels's "clever boys"—were particularly adept at dodging the Federal Armed Forces. Not only were they cleverer in their deceits, but because being accepted to the university in West Berlin was the easiest and—at least initially—safest way to avoid service. The Abitur, the exam that qualifies for university, provided a turning point, usually coinciding with moving out of the parental home and bringing increased mobility for the soon-to-be students, right at a crucial moment—unlike the apprentices, who usually were much younger. While apprentices faced military conscription amid their working life, those leaving secondary school were already facing the decision of where to go and to which university. Right at that point in their lives, one city was particularly appealing: Berlin!

One of them was Carsten from Gifhorn. In school, Carsten had been an absolute anarchist, pushed every possible button, with his "mat" of hair hanging far down over his denim jacket, and often an open bottle of Wittinger Pilsner under his desk in the classroom. He had somehow managed to reach a state of peaceful coexistence with his teachers in his final year in secondary school, but the Federal Armed Forces who would treat him like a slave? No way would he survive that, he was sure. And the alternative, civilian service? He didn't buy into this at all. So, he headed to West Berlin.

Since the mid-1960s, the half-city was particularly appealing to the Left. The Vietnam War created many pacifists, which is why personal aversion to military service was best based on political grounds. This led to the formation of a unique sociotope in West Berlin. The legendary Kommune 1 and other relevant circles in the leftist scene recruited, in no small measure, young men who had set out to avoid conscription. Manfred Grashof was one, but not the only one to move to Berlin to avoid the Federal Armed Forces, who later became a militant RAF fighter. Heinrich Lummer, the Berlin senator of the interior and a CDU-hardliner, was still worried in 1985 that Berlin would become an "oasis of non-compliance for dodgers" and called for a mandatory year of social service to prevent that from happening.

Their legal position was not as clear, however, as the Berlin refugees imagined. At first, the date of the conscription notice was the determining factor, of the summons to be present with toothbrush in hand at a specific barracks on a specific date. Those who changed their residence to West Berlin before that summons were usually in the clear. In the sixties, the German Federal Parliament changed the National Service Act. Once registered—at the tender age of 17—young men were subject to military monitoring. Changes in residence required permission from the district recruiting office under the scope of compulsory military service. Relocations to West Berlin were included. And permission was generally denied.

Even for the "clever ones," those who had already changed their residence before their military registration—the high school students with years to go before their Abitur—the hurdles got higher. The determining factor was no longer their official residence, but their "permanent address" instead, which for students was the same as their parents' residence. So, that green Berlin ID card no longer provided immunity from registration, mustering, conscription—or, unfortunately, from the military police behind the bush at the Helmstedt border crossing either.

Only absconding tied the hands of the military officials. By order of the Allies, once the conscripted recruits fled to West Berlin, federal officials could no longer enlist the help of the judiciary there to capture them and send them back to federal territory, as it had occurred two or three times in the 1960s. They could not officially send notifications for either mustering or conscription to Berlin—also because of Allied restrictions. To sidestep this problem, the district recruiting offices resorted to an unbureaucratic trick: The authority of the notification no longer lay in the posted writ of summons, but in the addressee's expected, careless response.

Individual employees in the district offices began to use their private return addresses and write in their own hands what at first glance appeared to be personal letters to the military refugees in Berlin. The content: conscription notice. The calculation behind it on the part of the merry letter writers: brash renegades would see such a letter as a provocation, a challenge to reply with angry or snarky words and send the notice back—with a misplaced sense of untouchability inside the walled city of West Berlin.

If they gave in to this temptation, the district recruitment office had confirmation of delivery in hand, and the conscription was legally binding. And at that point, whoever did not come voluntarily really did see the military police waiting for him at Helmstedt the next time he traveled back to the West. Or they knocked on the parents' door during semester breaks. Or the girlfriend's.

So, Bernd Schaper and his friend Ulf Merten received their strange letters from Braunschweig. They, however, refrained from any type of haughty response, because their attorney, steeled by many years of experience, had warned them. And so they remained undisturbed. It helped that they had not only moved to West Berlin but had also submitted requests for conscientious-objector status. According to the legal situation in the early 1970s, a court of law was required to rule on the matter. As the appointed date approached, of which the court in Braunschweig had notified them—again in a handwritten envelope—both did as their attorney had advised them: they informed the court of a "procedural impediment"—their domicile in Berlin. The date was repealed, and four months later, so was the entire proceeding.

Because both had successfully torpedoed their own proceedings, logic then would have required the Federal Armed Forces to immediately push for their conscription again. Why didn't that happen? Apparently, the Federal Ministry of Defense left undisturbed those openly unwilling to serve, in light of the surplus of recruits that was obvious at the time, though they never officially confirmed it.

Later, in the final years of compulsory service, after the fall of the Wall and in the Internet Age, there was lively discussion on what methods remained for dodging conscription, after the trick with West Berlin no longer worked in the reunited Germany. Many half-truths circulated online. Some would work at one district recruiting office but not another, and generally everything was to be taken with a grain of salt. Like the rumor that anyone who had completed a third of the standard period of study could not be conscripted (and brewery studies required only four semesters). Or the one about tattooing swastikas on one's arse, for which the district recruiting offices—concerned about radical right-wing activity—would immediately deem the bearer "unfit."

Perhaps not completely impossible, but how would one rid oneself of those swastikas? Or the tip in the chat about illnesses that are difficult to verify: Tinnitus—just gonna put that out there." Whether someone claiming to be gay would be kept out of the troops was also disputed in the scene. "They'll be drafted and then are usually put in a troop all by themselves," one warned, claiming to be in the know. Occasionally there was sage advice, like the warning not to be overly rash in pretending to have an infirmity at the mustering, for example, to which this suggestion applied: "Be careful. What you pretend or disclose there can have unfortunate consequences later, for disability insurance."

The medical examination was a crapshoot anyway: One might get his longtime family doctor on his side, who might have been a conscientious objector himself and issues a doctor's note about back pain or dizzy spells for the muster, while the other gets a doctor who fought on the eastern front and would love to send all dodgers up for court martial.

For many years, Bernd and Ulf weren't sure whether they were really in the clear, because their conscriptions were never officially revoked. At the time, it was said that no one would be drafted once they reached the age of 33. But that did not appear anywhere in writing, and they still had many years to go. That tingling sensation when, after the Vopo checkpoint on the east side, the west border agent asked for their ID, persisted. Once it led to severe heart palpitations, when the border guard asked, "Well, young men, which of you still has to go to the military?" For four, five seconds he smirked in silence before returning their IDs and saying, "Have a good trip," and laughing his head off with his partner next to him. Since then, the tingling at the border has been more bearable. It was all just a joke.

Ulli Kulke, born in 1952, lives as a reporter and author in Berlin. Until 2016, he was employed by Die Welt, *after he was a staff writer for* taz, Natur, Wochenpost *and the magazine* Mare. *He wrote pieces for magazines, including* SZ *and* ZEIT magazines, Playboy, National Geographic, FAZ *and* Der Spiegel. *His main focus as a book author is the history of discovery and lunar travel. Photo: Weber*

Helmstedt 172 km
Berlin-Mitte
200
m

Transit to Wessiland

By Tanja Dückers

We usually left West Berlin by car. Our mother always drove, because our father never got his driver's license; perhaps a good decision, as nobody could well imagine this imaginative, sensitive person at the wheel of a car.

Most of the time we went to the Dreilinden-Drewitz border crossing (we just said Dreilinden, the transit point in West Berlin), that is, to the tank. The tank was standing just before the GDR checkpoint, so it greeted us. The tank was positioned so that its gun barrel was pointed at West Berlin. We children understood this symbolic language, and our parents would talk about it often and with a lot of discomfort. The war vehicle placed here was the first Russian tank to reach Berlin in 1945. The Soviet military administration had erected this "landmark," here, after several relocations starting in 1969.

Once we reached Dreilinden, we had plenty of time to look at the tank, because we had to wait—always—for ages. I found the tank as impressive as it was frightening. We children pestered our parents with questions, but they knew little about such things. Our father had avoided the draft because he was nearsighted. One of my favorite quartet games I played as a schoolgirl did not involve cats or horses, but tanks. Even today, I can surprise many a former draftee or soldier with knowledge about the Tiger, the Leopard 2, or some or the other artillery piece ("self-propelled gun" I added to my list of favorite words).

The older I got, the less scary the tank seemed; it had aged a bit with the Cold War that was dragging on endlessly. In December 1990, the tank was lifted from its pedestal by the departing Soviet troops, and taken away. Since 1992, a pink snow loader has stood on its old spot, at the initiative of sculptor Eckhardt Haisch. It was a special construction based on the Soviet GAZ 69 all-terrain vehicle.

As West Berliners who often travelled to West Germany, we thought of ourselves as inhabitants of a third planet. Nothing was stranger than suddenly being called a Wessi (short for West German) after the fall of the Wall. My grandparents, my cousins, and some of our uncles and aunts were Wessis. Wessis were people from another world who had to cross two borders to visit us. The country they came from was called BRD or West Germany—the country we lived in was called Berlin. On a vacation trip to Cornwall, UK with my parents, I persistently repeated that I was not from Germany, but from Berlin. We didn't say West Berlin, but Berlin. It was obvious that we did not live in East Berlin, otherwise we would not be playing badminton in Cornwall.

The prejudice that was cultivated in Berlin against Wessis probably roughly corresponds to what big city dwellers generally think of country bumpkins. The fact that many West Berliners were often provincial themselves was something we ignored. Berlin before the fall of the Wall had had a cozy, not quite cosmopolitan atmosphere, and God knows it was not daring and cool all over. Furthermore, we Berliners overlooked the fact that there are great differences in the degree of provinciality between a resident of Hamburg, Cologne or Munich and one from, let's say, Oberneumais, Feuerschützenbostel or Kleinbockedra.

Berliners liked to make gross generalizations, not only about the habitus, but also about the assumed inner life of the Wessis. We assumed, I have to admit, that West Germans lived under a rock. We didn't realize that they thought the same of us, living encircled by the GDR, behind a wall, if not on the back side of the moon. In a provocative reversal of the real circumstances, we West Berliners called West Germany "Restdeutschland". Rest instead of West—but the word "rest" in German doesn't mean "pause" or "break." It actually means "leftovers."

On top of this, the Wessis, according to a widely held opinion among the cool people in West Berlin, had little taste. They only liked the picturesque, the comfortable, or the completely unbearable. There was the son of our grandparents' car dealer in Münster, who worked at a bank and would actually walk around wearing a wide Scrooge-McDuck tie. On the tie, Scrooge could be seen jumping into a pile of gold coins. I assume there were people like that in Berlin too, yet they seemed to confirm a stereotype. The Wessis in my generation still had old-fashioned names. All the Ulrichs, Ulfs, Udos, Wolfgangs, Lothars and Kläuse, the Hildegards, Sigruns, Ingeborgs, Dagmars and Hannelores came, of course, from West Germany.

If the West Germans weren't provincial, then they were radical punks—mohawk wearers—or crazy guys who, in neurotic permanent rebellion against their Geranium-and-Mercedes-Benz parents' homes, were not to be taken too seriously politically. After running riot in Berlin for a while, they would either dutifully move back to Mannheim or

Fürstenfeldbruck to start a family, maybe to their grandparents' house, or they would end up doing heroin back in the city, and kill themselves.

In any case, it was a shock for me to suddenly be called a "Wessi" after the fall of the Wall. There is hardly a West Berliner who doesn't defend himself against it to this day.

Our ignorance of West Germany acquired during the Wall era would rear its head later. Entire German states remained blank spots on my inner map. It was significant that by the age of twelve I could recite all the states of the USA, Canada (I liked names like Manitoba and Saskatchewan, as well as Yukon) and Australia, but failed with the German equivalents.

The Wessis, for their part, believed we were living in the "deep East," just outside of the Ural Mountains. The time it took us to get to any West German city was usually overestimated. But it certainly took some time to leave Berlin and arrive in West Germany, and that was mainly due to the wait at the border. This long wait took up a lot of our lives.

Once we had reached the queues of cars, the usual game began: everyone thought that this or that queue was making particularly rapid progress. Whenever our mother had just changed lanes, the fast line would stop moving, as if frozen forever, in time, in motion, in everything. Then we would change lines, only for the process to repeat itself. We were always developing new theories—usually wrong ones—about which line would move the fastest. Once, my mother put herself right at the end of the longest queue, which I thought was a bit fatalistic—she had had enough of our theories. In those days, cars with air conditioning were rare, and at 95 degrees Fahrenheit it could get pretty uncomfortable during the summer vacations.

The proof of this was provided by the many ARAL car atlases curled by the heat, which lay behind the seats in every other car, stewing away next to a roll of toilet paper. And there were no computer games or consoles for us kids yet, while we waited endlessly at the border.

In the seventies, many drivers started saving gas. This was in the years after the oil crisis, when Willy Brandt's Socialdemocratic-Liberal government had decided on a total of four car-free Sundays, as well as on speed limits. We walked in amazement through the urban space that was suddenly available for us. We could walk on the Avus autobahn, on Heerstrasse, everywhere where pedestrians had previously been treated like criminals. How wide the streets were! How much space was available to cars every day!

We pedestrians understood at that moment that the cities had long since assigned us a secondary role. The sidewalks still flank the streets in a gesture of humility. The center, the center belongs to the cars; we, the pedestrians, always give way to the edge for them. Yet the infrastructure owed to traffic, which we now consider almost natural, is not even a hundred years old. As is well known, Europe's first traffic light shone at Potsdamer Platz in Berlin in 1924.

I later went to many rallies with witty papier-mâché figures, crazy costumes, funny banners, and wild bands, but those car-free Sundays, when nothing happened but completely normal pedestrians walking peacefully across the street, had the most impressive "accessory": the emptiness, the square, the air, the absence of traffic noise, the awareness that today we were here, where otherwise only cars had been.

And so, at that time, travelers in transit also began to get out of their cars and push them instead of driving. Did that shorten the waiting time? No, but at least you were outside, in the more or less fresh air.

The prejudices between West Berliners and Wessis existed, as I mentioned, on both sides. There was an elderly aunt who asked my brother and me during a family visit if we always had to carry a knife in our pocket, because Berlin was so dangerous: drugs, Christiane F. (a famous drug addict whose life story was made into a film), gangs of some kind, squatters, left-wing politicians!

The West Germans were also always afraid that West Berlin could be sealed off by the Russians—that's why only few relatives came to visit us. There was the singular visit from a West German uncle and aunt, who, of course, arrived at Bahnhof Zoo. In those days, they traveled on old Reichsbahn trains that took six and a half hours from Berlin to Münster (today: three and a half hours).

Zoologischer Garten Station, or Bahnhof Zoo for short, located at the Berlin zoo, had opened in 1882, but was not extended for mainline rail until the 1936 Berlin Olympics. During the war, it had been severely damaged. But after the closure of all the other long-distance stations, it emerged as the only train station in the walled city. And although it only had two platforms for long-distance traffic, it became, for decades, West Berlin's most important rail hub.

Bahnhof Zoo, the Zoo Station, was the starting point for interzonal and transit trains to the federal territory, for transit passengers who did not want to, or could not, travel by car. And it was an institution. Tall, dark and dingy, it had a gloomy, lofty aura. A new, clean, uncluttered station could not have had such an atmosphere. That Bahnhof Zoo would one day be downgraded to a regional station was beyond the realm of imagination. Many older West Berliners still feel this as a serious insult today.

My uncle and aunt from West Germany, however, did not consider Bahnhof Zoo an institution, let alone a lofty one. Already on their way to the parking lot, they were appalled by the many bums. They said something like: "there are more and more of them here! Back then, the vagrants were war-disabled, and we had pity on them, but today…,"

They got a whimsical answer back from us: "today, they are no longer war-disabled, but capitalism-disabled." The sight of the big Beate-Uhse sex store, with sex films and related articles as well as the ugly food stalls at the zoo, did not improve their impression of West Berlin.

Uncle and aunt luckily didn't stay with us in our peculiar furnished home, filled with abstract paintings and sculptures and indistinguishable "works of art" by my brother and me, but instead in a posh hotel nearby. On their last night, our parents asked: "So what were your impressions of Berlin?" Our strong-minded uncle, ever eager to discuss things, immediately had a harsh view ready to deploy: "You live in a dying city! Not even at the end of the war could Berlin have been sadder than it is now!" After this assertion, an exhausting discussion developed. Uncle and aunt were not to be dissuaded from their opinion. Berlin would fall to the Soviet Union, West Berlin was an absurd construct anyway, and in the long run this remnant would be far too expensive for the federal government to keep. And here were only "silly kids looking for adventures," trying to manifest themselves in Berlin.

Our father objected. He was, after all, the director of the Kupferstichkabinett, an art museum—this probably screamed "adult kid looking for adventure" to our uncle and aunt. He believed that the Americans would not leave West Berlin "to the Russian," and that they had done quite a bit for Berlin—keyword "airlift." My uncle and aunt, however, disregarded this. "The Russian" would not look idly at the morsel under his nose for another thirty years, but would eventually bite. "The Russian" was ponderous, sluggish, and patient, and if he attacked West Berlin, or simply sealed off the borders, we'd all be looking down the tubes. The Americans would certainly not send troops "because of you". And if there were a nuclear war, which our self-assured aunt assumed would surely happen sooner rather than later, then we would be living in a dying city!

Then they sped away again from Zoo Station to their boring town of Leverkusen. We were left with their gloomy predictions. Our parents tried to dispel any worries—"this is not a dying city, it's the liveliest place in Germany!"—but when I stood at the window in my room late at night and looked at our backyard, at the old skeletonized bicycle racks, the dented garbage cans, the garbage lying around, and the rats jumping out of the garbage cans, I wasn't so sure they were right.

At the old dingy Bahnhof Zoo, however, I felt that my father had a point: despite even the hookers, the drunks, and the perpetual peeing on the wall at the stinking Zoo, there was something that made you not believe that this city couldn't die just like that. Berlin somehow always felt good, even if it didn't look pretty—especially on its ugly corners.

When it was finally our car's turn at the Dreilinden border control point, the GDR personnel were almost never friendly. But this was, perhaps, due little to any political bias against us. Several times our parents tried to explain or justify to us children the unfriendly, condescending, and breathtakingly monotonous behavior of the GDR-border troops with their "terribly boring job". Occasionally, our parents also consoled us by saying that East Germans had always had to wait so long for everything. In the East, they had to wait to go shopping, to go to a restaurant, to buy a car, to rent an apartment—always waiting—and we were only waiting today, right now, in line at the border crossing.

"Does 'Wartburg' come from waiting?" my brother once mused jokingly. The German word "warten" (to wait) seemed to have something to do with this East German car, my younger brother assumed. And our father answered: "I wouldn't mind the long wait if you got something good at the end, but the food, the cars, the clothes, it's all … all gray … bland."

"Did you buy your gray suit in the East?" my brother asked, and our father had to grin.

"Haaach, you, you're a little pain in the ass;" turning back to his newspaper on the passenger seat.

Once we were finally through the checkpoint, the transit route, cobbled together from concrete slabs, lay gray and seemingly endless before us. Immediately, the highway felt different; at intervals of about hundred and fifty feet we drove over broken asphalt, to the sound of a monotonous rumble. The colors of the traffic signs were lighter, paler. And only a speed of sixty-two miles per hour was allowed. From today's perspective, the GDR was actually progressive in this respect, even if not for ecological reasons. However, it did increase driving time considerably. And while the West had rest areas with brightly lit bungalows, here we found only a few basic seats. Back in the car, the opaque front of green and anthracite pines flew by again outside.

The two-and-a-half-hour drive to the Helmstedt border crossing felt like forever: pines, pines, pines, pale signs, lines of cars, the fractures in the asphalt, the occasional large block of houses in the distance, industry. Only when we drove past the sign reading "Magdeburg" did something change. Each time, our mother would exclaim with glee, "Look, the Magdeburg Cathedral!"

And the three of us would synchronously turn our heads in the cathedral's direction. There was something as imposing as it was eerie about the way the two towers of the church loomed somberly and hugely over the landscape. It reminded me of the Kaiser Wilhelm Memorial Church in West Berlin's center. This church, destroyed in the Second World

War, had been left as a ruin after the end of the war, and now functioned as a memorial.

Although we regarded the West Germans with condescension, we didn't really have many opportunities of contact with the East either: I had only been there a few times, with my parents, with the school on

our hiking day, when visitors came to Berlin. Every trip to East Berlin was dominated by conflicting feelings: is it terrible here?! Is it beautiful here?! The colors were missing; streets, shop windows, cars, and faces were of a strange pallor. The food lacked spices. But there was the old famous boulevard Unter den Linden, the main cathedral, the Brandenburg Gate—wasn't the heart of Berlin in the East? You could definitely sense that as a child. A half city was waiting here that had a strange resemblance to ours and yet seemed completely foreign. And the people were Berliners!

We hardly understood the Bavarians or the Swabians, but the East Berliners, who lived in a different political system behind the Wall, spoke quite similarly to us (despite the subtle differences between East Berlin and West Berlin dialect). That was irritating. I must admit, I never felt comfortable in the East. Because of the constant oscillation between a sense of closeness and a sense of foreignness, I could never really relax. When you were there, you were never in just one place, but mentally and emotionally always in several places at the same time, geographically and on the time axis. Being in East Berlin felt like going back in time. Being there, one was stuck in a liminality, in an in-between place.

Actually, I've always loved to travel. As I got older, I developed a kind of wanderlust, or actually, one should say, local nostalgia. I remember the mother of a friend who had grown up in East Berlin and used to say things like: "the Zoo train station is sad today ... back then ... the Anhalter Bahnhof, the Schlesische Bahnhof—those were real stations with style! You don't know what Berlin looked like before the war."

At such moments, I was struck by how right she was. How different my hometown had looked a generation before I was born, before the Second World War, how foreign my own city was to me. But it bugged me, constantly having the feeling that I had missed the best of times in my hometown. The prevailing—often unspoken—feeling was: today's Berlin never can and never will come close to the Berlin of the Roaring Twenties. Berlin lived in a strangely post-aggressive mood of disgruntlement and melancholy.

Whenever we had been on vacation in West Germany— at our grandparents' in Münster or at the North Sea—we were always happy to see the sign "Helmstedt" on the way back. During the division of Germany, Helmstedt was the most important crossing point between the Federal Republic and the GDR, but also the western terminus of one of the transit routes to West Berlin. During the GDR era, little Helmstedt had gained a tremendous amount of notoriety. And there we were again, enveloped in a cloud of exhaust gas, waiting.

Finally, we were allowed to move up. A bored soldier whose complexion was as gray as his uniform looked at us with suspicion and condescension. Please don't turn the car upside down again and unscrew the hubcaps, we thought .... a longer look at the passport of our father with his long hair, then we were through. When we had left the transit route behind us, high spirits would erupt for a moment. Finally on the Avus: it was no longer necessary to drive at a speed of sixty miles, our mother accelerated elatedly, and the speedometer of our old rickety Benz climbed to ninety miles per hour. Soon we were home!

Every time we crossed that border, a little weight would fall off our shoulders—as if somewhere, in the back of our minds, we were afraid that one day we might find it blocked, stopping us from getting back home to West Berlin.

Tanja Dückers was born in 1968 in West Berlin. Today she lives with her family in East Berlin. She has published twenty books. As a journalist, she writes about cultural and sociopolitical topics for various German newspapers. She has lived in the USA many times as a writer-in-residence or lecturer. Since 2016 she has been working for different projects working with refugee-writers. *Photo: Anton Landgraf*

Adventures in Plänterwald

By Andreas Austilat

We were nineteen or twenty years old and from West Berlin. Maybe that explains what we did, because, well, we misbehaved. That's probably also why I had kind of forgotten about this story. And I'd kept it that way up until that day in 2014 when the Spreepark burnt down—the Spreepark, which we had once called the Plänterwald. In the newspapers, we read a couple of things about the only amusement park in the GDR, the German Democratic Republic, how East Germany was officially named, and most of all, how much of a bummer it was that it seemed forever lost. Well, to be honest, back then in 1977, it wasn't exactly pure amusement that awaited us there.

It started with our entry to East Berlin—this turned out to be tricky. The procedure went as follows: a couple of days prior, we had gone to an East German Pass Office called Passierscheinbüro—there were several of those exterritorial missions in West Berlin—and picked up our warrant to visit East Berlin as West Berliners. As an entry document, we had to show a "Behelfsmäßigen Personalausweis," a makeshift ID card. It was green and quite different from those grey document the West Germans had. This ID card was important for the authorities of the GDR because, as West Berliners, we were not officially citizens of the Federal Republic of Germany, as West Germany was formally named. We stood on our own as inhabitants of a small island in the east, surrounded by a wall, guarded by American, British, and French forces. Besides the ID, we had to have an explanation for our planned entry. The preferred explanation over there—we actually called the East "over there"—was: "Berlin, capital of the GDR, as a tourist." This sounded funny because we had our own Berlin, which was not the capital of anything in those days. Nevertheless, I wrote that explanation down word for word.

It wasn't all too clear to me what we actually wanted over there.

I'd only been to East Berlin once: to visit the Pergamon Museum of Ancient Middle Eastern Art, together with my aunt. That must have been in 1972, shortly after the Four Power Agreement, which had suddenly made it possible for us to enter. In fact, before that, it hadn't been easy to get to East Berlin as a West Berliner. Well, I don't want to be unfair: the other way around wasn't possible at all.

My only memory from that visit to the Pergamon Museum was that they didn't have real Coke. A fifteen-year-old remembers something like that. But this time we planned to have fun for cheap. For one West-Mark

we could probably get eight East-Mark. The only question was where to have fun. And how should we spend the enormous amount of money in our pockets? That's what led us to the Plänterwald, the only permanent amusement park between us and the Tivoli in Copenhagen. To be fair, there was also the Heidepark Soltau in West Germany, but we only ever went there with our parents.

In West Berlin, we also had an Oktoberfest, which wasn't the same as the real one in Munich, and which seemed kind of depressing to me with its brass band imitation. The German American Volksfest was great, since the USA seemed like it was on another planet—this was before the era of cheap flights. We got to see real Americans there. They had "Michelob," real American beer, and American ice cream. Those were pretty "cool," as we already used to say.

Meanwhile, in the Plänterwald, we could go on the rollercoaster as many times as we wanted, whereas it was an expensive luxury in West Berlin. They had bumper cars called "Auto-Arena" and a "Kosmodrom," a spiderlike thing with little carts. Alright then, the Plänterwald; what other thing was there to do on an afternoon in East Berlin?

There were three of us: Tom, whose nickname was Schummel, Chris, and I, and we arrived in a pretty big Citroen DS Safari, a station wagon that belonged to Chris' mother. Citroen DS, that's the one they nicknamed "shark mouth." The appearance we made at the border crossing Bornholmer Strasse was without question a provocative one. This aside, the control went relatively smoothly, up until the moment when Schummel posed the silly question of where the coerced exchange was. Back then, it was 6,50 West-Mark that had to be exchanged for the price of one for one into East-Mark. The East German Vopo—the common abbreviation for Volkspolizist—seemed shocked, and asked whether Schummel meant the minimum exchange, to which my friend unfortunately responded: "coerced, minimum, doesn't matter, isn't it the all same anyways?"

Yes, we were young. Schummel was quite sturdy, and looked a bit weird. He always wore a black suit and yellow glasses, yellow shoes, and a Hawaiian shirt. The Vopo turned to me and asked: "is this man with you?"

It was absolutely clear that we were in trouble, particularly as the guard started to adopt a straddle-legged stance, which only showed off his uniform more, with its high boots and sort of riding pants. I slowly began to explain that I was only driving. "Well then, go ahead and drive and pull over to the right," he said. By this he meant a special lane, exclusively for us.

Unfortunately, they immediately found the baton in the door. I was still trying to figure out how it had ended up there. It wasn't my car; Chris' older brother usually used it. The Vopo took the baton and asked, "and what's this?" That's when he reminded me that I had already been asked if I had any "weapons, radio devices, or ammunition" on us, a standard question posed when we Westerners passed across the GDR border. And as always, we had responded with "no."

"This truncheon is a weapon," the Vopo said into my silence. I considered what to do in case the situation should escalate. There wasn't any ambassador I could have asked to talk to. There was a "Permanent Representation of the Federal Republic of Germany," but I had no idea whether it was responsible for West Berliners. I wasn't even allowed to elect the Bundestag—that only became legal in 1990 after reunification. "This is not my car," I said, which sparked a longer lecture, as the man started to question who I really was. A provocateur, the answer emerged. In fact, we aroused the suspicion of being a band of provocateurs.

The Vopo grew more and more enraged, up until the point where he must have assumed that I'd been out beating up the unemployed West Berlin masses with the thing. This I found pretty unfair. I was a student and politically rather left, much like all the other students I'd known. It was for this reason that I couldn't think of anything to say about the stick. Not that it was necessary because, at that very moment, a second Vopo emerged from the other side, and asked again: "and what's this?" He was holding a coin, twenty centimes, which he had found in the door's side pocket.

"Twenty French centimes," I answered, happy about this distraction. "That's five cents, if anything."

"That's foreign currency," the Vopo said, "which you should have indicated."

I offered to throw the coin away directly, which of course wasn't allowed. I was eventually given the option to throw it into a donation box. I believe it was for the reconstruction of the People's Republic of Vietnam.

While Chris was made to remove the door panel, I was led into a shed for further questioning. There I had to empty out my pockets. Right away, I felt the condom in the breast pocket of my denim jacket. No, that wasn't mine, either. I had taken it from my sixteen-year-old tutoring student a few days before. I left it in my pocket, but of course, I had to remove the jacket itself, and the Vopo declared in response to finding it: "so you're in the capital as a tourist."

Afterwards, I had to go through my phonebook with him, page after page. We stopped at the letter D for a while, D for Waclaw Dajnowiec, whom I had met at a Swedish campground during summer vacation. Back then, there was no Facebook or anything like that, which is why we had exchanged addresses... on paper. "Is this man citizen of the People's Republic of Poland?" I said yes. The Poles were already allowed to travel into neutral Sweden. "When did you last see him? Where? Did he give you anything? Did you give him anything?" At that moment I no longer wanted to enter the capital of the GDR, but to go home to my cozy West Berlin. Adieu, Plänterwald.

Schummel had it even worse. He negligently stated that he wanted to

visit his aunt. She lived in East Berlin, and we had planned to exchange money with her. East Berliners were very interested in western currencies, which allowed them to buy western goods in special shops. Now he was being asked her name and where she lived, which he didn't want to say because he feared her getting into trouble. Schummel said: "I don't know. I only call her Aunt Bärbel." And he also didn't really know where she lived—he was only able to describe the house. They brought out a street map of East Berlin, and he was asked to locate the place. Schummel sat there, motionlessly, for about an hour, and every ten minutes, when the Vopo came, he would say, "sorry, I can't find it."

I didn't expect them to let us enter anymore. But they did. All I had left to do was remount the door of the Citroen. We actually did end up visiting Schummel's aunt, and exchanged some money for the bogus black market price. And then we eventually arrived at the Plänterwald.

They say that after its foundation in 1969, the Plänterwald had had around 1.5 million visitors per year. As I said, we arrived there in the afternoon, but we were nevertheless surprised by how empty the culture park seemed to us—that's what it was called officially. Not necessarily cool, that's for sure. Fine, the renowned Ferris wheel had already been built, although it was a bit smaller than the one-hundred-forty-feet to come in 1989. Most of the apparatuses, which were only installed during the 1990s, ended up originating from the assets of a bankrupt

French amusement park. They didn't yet exist in 1977. The city scenery that burnt down towards the end of the nineties didn't exist either, but came much later. The only chassis that would have been attractive for us—remember, this was 1977—was the roller coaster, a real and already older version of the "Alpen Express." But it was out of order. Apparently there had been an accident.

We wandered aimlessly around the broad pavement. Since the area

was so spacious, it looked like there were only a few stalls. Somehow any sort of funfair music was also missing, noticeable in spite of the humorous announcers trying to keep the crowd cheerful. Every few minutes, there'd be something like: "uh-oh now ready for some speed!" or "Heads up! The next round is going backwards!" At some point, we stopped at a raffle ticket booth. We still had our pockets full of money we couldn't find a way to get rid of.

Schummel asked the ticket seller whether she'd be able to close if we bought the bucket full of tickets. "No," she said, "I'd get a new bucket." We bought two buckets and won the first prize, a bottle of real Martini Vermouth, as well as a game of morris and some smaller prizes.

Then I approached the shooting gallery. I didn't hit anything. At this point, the man behind the counter clearly identified us as West Berliners. It wasn't the dialect. In fact, we didn't sound much different from him. He probably just took us for snobs. However, as he watched my failure, he suddenly remarked: "you learned this at the Bundeswehr, huh." Bundeswehr was the official name of the West German army.

I think it was all just too much. I had been taken apart multiple times that day, accused simultaneously of being a provocateur and a currency smuggler. Moreover, I was a West Berliner, demilitarized. We weren't drafted into any army. I bought lots of ammunition for ten East-Mark and shot at the booth erratically. It was like a drumroll. Afterwards, I said: "that's what superiority in material looks like."

The Plänterwald and I; we never saw each other again. In fact, I forgot about it. Meanwhile, it burnt to the ground.

Andreas Austilat, born in Berlin-Lichterfelde, is a reporter for Der Tagesspiegel, *where his column "Austilat spart sich's" appears regularly. He has published several books, among them* Hotel kann jeder *about the joys of camping,* Vom Winde gesät, *about gardening and* Mark Twain in Berlin. *His last book is* Auch das geht vorbei, *a book about men navigating their midlife crisis.* *Photo: Mike Wolff*

BERLINER GEDENKTAFEL
In diesem Haus wohnte von 1976 bis 1978
DAVID BOWIE
8.1.1947 – 10.1.2016
In dieser Zeit entstanden die Alben »Low«, »Heroes«
und »Lodger«. Sie gingen als Berliner Trilogie
in die Musikgeschichte ein
»We can be heroes, just for one day«
Gefördert durch die GASAG Berliner Gaswerke Aktiengesellschaft
MARYCULA

Heroes on Hauptstrasse

By Paul Hockenos

The West Berlin, in which the London-born David Robert Jones, alias David Bowie, arrived in 1976, was the city of Bahnhof Zoo. Shortly after Bowie's arrival, a teenage girl named Christiane Felscherinow catapulted the city's central train station, and 1970s West Berlin with it, into the all-time annals of decadence and excess. Felscherinow was a junkie and part-time hooker who sniffed her first line of heroin at the age of thirteen. Under the name Christiane F. she told her bleak, but engrossing story in a 1978-published memoir *Wir Kinder vom Bahnhof Zoo*, which became an international bestseller, also published in the United States, and a cult biopic three years later.

Berlin in the 1970s wasn't a pulsating, Weimar-era-inspired sanctum of transsexual decadence and artistic ferment, as Bowie seems to have believed—or hoped. The Weimar Republic's offbeat revues and the dazzling pre-Nazi Berlin of Isherwood's novellas were, for the most part, buried deep beneath the war rubble. An expansive gay scene, the most feral in Germany, had reestablished itself soon after Nazi Germany's defeat, a graphic demonstration of the way subculture in Berlin can bounce back despite ferocious repression.

But the scene, even by the early 1970s, was closeted behind doors with buzzers and peepholes. The queer and punk rebellions of the near future were delicate buds just beginning to blossom in obscure niches. Bowie, though, looking to stumble onto fresh sources of inspiration, stepped into West Berlin at an auspicious moment, when a full-blown subcultural renaissance was in the offing. The West Berlin he'd leave would have more of the Golden Twenties about it than the one he entered. On the cusp of a new era, his person as well as his persona gave it a vigorous push.

Bowie's infatuation with Weimar-era culture and German expressionism in particular drew him to West Berlin in the first place. German films from the interwar years such as *Metropolis*, *M*, and *The Cabinet of Dr. Caligari* had captured his imagination years earlier. "Since my teenage years I had obsessed on the angst-ridden, emotional work of the expressionists, both artists and film makers, and Berlin had been their spiritual home," said Bowie in 1977.

Bowie had seen the film *Cabaret* several times. In 1975, on the Diamond Dogs world tour, he'd met Christopher Isherwood backstage in Los Angeles, and he peppered the writer, who was on a Buddhist retreat nearby, with questions about Berlin. In the photo of Bowie most associated with Berlin, he's dandied up in a 1920s black-and-white tux, bow tie, and short, slicked-back hair: a modern-day John Heartfield.

The thirty-year-old Bowie lived in the city from summer 1976 to autumn 1978, renting a spacious but otherwise prosaic finde-siècle apartment above a car-parts shop at 155 Hauptstrasse in Schöneberg, a loud thoroughfare in a district of avenues and parks a bike-ride south of Bahnhof Zoo, the Zoo station. Schöneberg was the heart of West Berlin's gay world, just as it had been in the interwar years. Isherwood had lived a twenty-minute walk from Bowie's address.

Bowie's name and his West Berlin labors are so closely linked to the city that forty years later a tourist bus schleps visitors around to the sites where the musician and his good friend Iggy Pop caroused back in the day. It makes stops at his former apartment on Hauptstrasse, the Hansa Studio, and the former location of Chez Romy Haag and the site of the now-long-defunct bar Dschungel. In West Berlin, in cooperation with the English musician and record producer Brian Eno, Bowie produced the so-called Berlin trilogy of albums: Low, Heroes, and Lodger, arguably his best work in a lifetime of making music. Bowie also co-wrote and produced Iggy Pop's albums "The Idiot and Lust for Life, some of Iggy's finest work in West Berlin. Bowie's single "Heroes" stands as an anthem of sorts for Berlin, a song purportedly inspired by a stealthy kiss along the Wall.

So hyped is Bowie's Berlin hiatus that some of the stories have become larger than life, at the expense of the facts. More than anything, though, Bowie's art of bending gender and fabricating identities—from Ziggy Stardust to the Thin White Duke, Major Tom to glam rock star—imbued West Berlin's subculture with fantasia that it riffed off of with verve. This is the case despite the fact that Bowie, while in West Berlin, dropped all of his alter egos and exotic costumes, and uncharacteristically played himself: painting, walking and cycling, writing songs. He dressed casually in jeans rolled up at the ankles, button-down shirts, and a 1950s-style golfer's cap.

One of the independent films from the day, the New German Cinema director Helke Sander's *The All-Around Reduced Personality* (German title *Die allseitig reduzierte Persönlichkeit—Redupers* (1977), includes slow, silent panning shots of West Berlin streetfronts filmed at the time Bowie lived there. It depicts forsaken neighborhoods along the Wall passed over by the economic miracle. There's no trace of the recovery that propelled the Federal Republic to the front of the industrial world. The film's Wall itself is largely unpainted, though randomly punctuated with sprayed slogans addressing the RAF or the Marxist splinter parties. Overgrown, trash-strewn lots and dead ends mark streets with buildings blackened by ash and soot. The handful of open shops have prewar-painted signs above their grimy windows such as "Laundry," "Coal Supplies," and "Groceries." Sander's sweeping shots of the neighborhoods bespeak squalor and emptiness.

This was the part of town where Christiane F. lived. Her story begins in the social housing project of Gropius City, an outlying suburb of West Berlin built in the 1960s along the Wall's westernmost perimeter.

Her family of four, having moved from the countryside in northern Germany, inhabit a drab two-and-a-half-room apartment on the eleventh floor of a building in the satellite suburb. The thirty-one-story cement Neubau (a newly built high-rise), the tallest in Germany at the time, was intended for lower-income families like the Felscherinows. In the early 1960s, this well-intentioned endeavor, ultimately an experiment

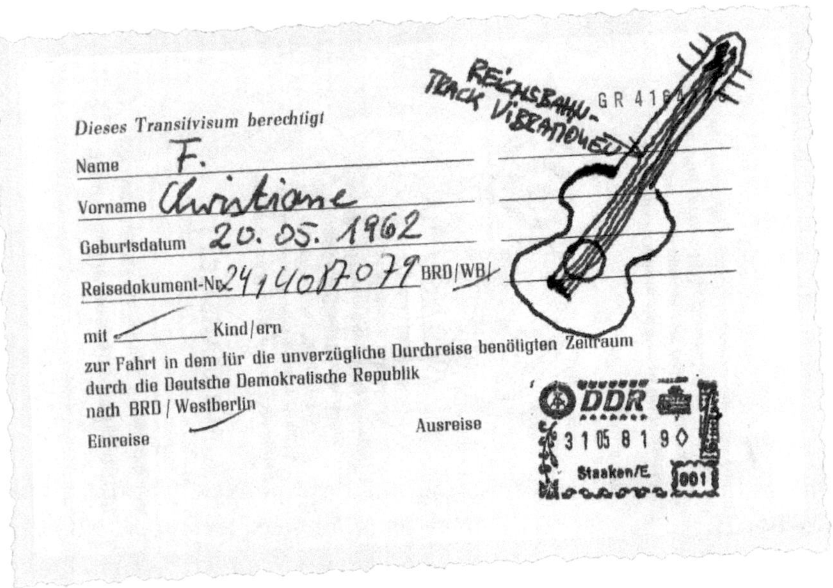

Dieses Transitvisum berechtigt

Name F.

Vorname Christiane

Geburtsdatum 20. 05. 1962

Reisedokument-Nr. 24140187079 BRD/WB

mit — Kind/ern

zur Fahrt in dem für die unverzügliche Durchreise benötigten Zeitraum durch die Deutsche Demokratische Republik nach BRD / Westberlin

Einreise

Ausreise

DDR 310581 90 Staaken/E. 001

in social engineering, was initially supervised by the prestigious architect Walter Gropius, a Hitler-era exile and in-the-meantime U.S. citizen. Today Gropius is celebrated as one of the founders of modern architecture. But the monstrosity that emerged from Gropius's blueprints was the product of an experiment gone terribly awry.

With extraordinary insight for a teenager, Felscherinow describes the grim underside of Wirtschaftswunder Germany, the miasma from which angry punk rock would emerge a few years later (and, soon after that, violent neo-Nazi cliques). Indeed, her critique of postwar German architecture reads like a script for the West Berlin band "Einstürzende Neubauten", literally "collapsing new buildings."

In order to escape it all, twelve-year-old Christiane starts smoking hash, and then dropping acid and popping pills with kids a bit older. The girls doll themselves up and head off to the downtown West Berlin disco Sound, which billed itself as "the most modern discothèque in Europe." Sound was a dark, gymnasium-like hall filled with bored and unkempt young adults on the prowl for sex or drugs or both, anything to kill the tedium. Christiane gets hooked on H and winds up with fellow child addicts along the underpasses and alleyways of the Bahnhof Zoo station. Their hangout is the Babystrich, the child prostitution scene, where johns cruise in search of underage flesh. Two tricks buy a fix. "Man," says Christiane's best pal, Babsi, "I gave seven blow jobs this morning and made 200 marks! That's a lot of dough!" A few weeks later Babsi overdoses, making her the city's youngest drug casualty ever.

The Babystrich, a red-light district, sleazy even by the standards of connoisseurs, flourished along Potsdamer Strasse, Kurfürstenstrasse, and around Nollendorfplatz. Prostitutes, pimps, gamblers, thugs, and drunks mixed in the rough quarter where stabbings and shootings were commonplace. At that time, West Berlin's red-light scene had the reputation of offering absolutely everything, one explorer from the era told me. And you didn't have to look far to find it. "It was wild," says Michael Sontheimer, a journalist who lived on Potsdamer Strasse and one morning nearly collided with a man naked but for a cowboy hat and boots striding out from one of the brothels.

Christiane and her sixteen-year-old boyfriend, Detlef, also a junkie, share a hovel of an apartment with another addict, Armin. A black-and-white picture of RAF member Ulrike Meinhof is taped up over the dingy mattress, a reminder that everything in late 1970s West Berlin happened against the backdrop of the German Autumn. When they find Armin dead, needle dangling from his arm, Christiane and Detlef run for it, leaving behind the garbage-littered room and bloodstained bedding. One after another, Christiane's peers overdose as she and Detlef float among johns' apartments, shooting galleries, police lockups, addict programs, and then back to the dealers and the sleaze of the Babystrich.

Christiane F.s memoir understandably staggered West Germany. (East Germany, on the other hand, felt vindicated by the sordid portrayal of life in capitalism's showcase.) What had West Germany's astounding economic recovery, the breakneck urban reconstruction, and half-hearted confrontation with the past made of its youngest generation? West Berlin was a cesspit, awash in narcotics, in which anything goes and no one cares, not even parents. The city's own statistics confirmed it: in 1977 alone, eighty-four people died of drug overdoses, more than in any other city in Europe. Even before the book's publication, Bowie seemed to know this, calling West Berlin "the heroin capital of Europe."

David Bowie is close to Christiane's heart and never far from her thoughts. In the film, she cherishes the "Changesonebowie" album like a security blanket and takes a drag on her first joint listening to Bowie. It's after a Bowie concert that she does her first line of heroin. The cool boys from her clique "look like David Bowie." David Bowie and his music are everything that Gropius City and her life aren't.

In terms of avant-garde brio, West Berlin was largely barren. The alternative movement had sown its seeds here and there, but you would have to search long and hard to find an art gallery. The seclusion and the slow pace, however, provided Bowie with the anonymity and peace of mind that eluded him in the United States and England. Even his neighbors didn't seem to give a damn who he was. So unimpressed were they about living next to one of the world's greatest rock stars, they called him "Mr. Boffie."

"Nobody was coming to West Berlin for any other reason than just to get away from somewhere else," explains Wolfgang Müller, an art school student in the 1970s and the impresario behind the band "Die Tödliche Doris" (Deadly Doris). I talked to Müller several times in his Kreuzberg walkup, a well-worn apartment he's been living in since the 1980s. It was Müller who suggested that I take a look at Sander's film, to get an idea of what 1970s West Berlin was like before the Wall was brightly painted. Müller decamped to West Berlin in the 1970s to get away from his industrial hometown of Wolfsburg. Wolfsburg was a city built by the Nazis for the purpose of manufacturing Hitler's automobile for the Volk, namely the Volkswagen. It was at the VW factory that Müller's father labored his life long, a fate Wolfgang Müller had no intention of replicating.

West Berlin's nightlife may not have been flashy, but it boasted gay bars aplenty and lesbian hangouts, too—more than any other German city. What made West Berlin attractive for gay men such as Müller, as well as lesbians and transsexuals, was its remoteness, far away and sealed off as it was from the Federal Republic. And the Berlin natives, though known for cranky demeanors, were less ruffled by nonconformist lifestyles than most western Germans. But until the end of the 1970s, says Müller, gay culture in West Berlin happened largely behind closed doors. The seventy or so establishments for gay men had buzzers and peepholes. A doorperson would admit select customers into closet-sized bars and backroom discos that looked straight out of Rainer Werner Fassbinder's film *Fox and His Friends* (The German title is *Faustrecht der Freiheit,* 1975) which portrays this milieu in seedy detail.

Their patrons kept pretty much to their own kind. "Men weren't allowed in lesbian clubs, for example, or leather gays in trans bars," says Müller. Yet many decades passed before their equivalent arose in other European metropolises, there were same-sex bars, dance halls, transvestite balls, and much more. Darkrooms were routine in clubs such as Mister X and Hoppla Sir, which attracted gay tourists like metal filings to a magnet for exactly that purpose. And the fact that West Berlin had no closing hour was icing on the cake.

It's often impossible to pinpoint the threads that lead from present-day Berlin back to the interwar era, so thoroughly did the Nazis blot them out. But the city's gay culture has a strong link to the past. Despite the Third Reich's brutal suppression of homosexuality, it rebounded remarkably quickly in the city, where, according to historian Robert Beachy in *Gay Berlin: Birthplace of a Modern Identity,* homosexual identity was born in the late nineteenth century and flourished until the 1930s. Berlin was known for its more liberal treatment of same-sex erotic love long before the era of Weimar. Beachy claims that the concept of Schwul, or "gay," didn't even exist in London or New York before it was parlance in Berlin.

In the early 1970s, a love interest brought twenty-three-year-old Romy Haag to West Berlin, a city that the transsexual performer had long been linked to—even though she'd never been there. In Paris, at clubs like the legendary Alcazar de Paris, she was introduced as "the sensational Romy Haag, straight from Berlin!" Apparently, it was thought to sound more risqué than Amsterdam. After the thrilling nocturnal splendor of the nightclubs of Paris and New York, Haag was as appalled as Wolfgang Müller at the quality of West Berlin's nightlife. The red-light district, notes Haag scornfully in her autobiography, was the only place where—and context in which—you could find transsexuals in West Berlin. She'd change that.

Born as Edouard Frans Verbaarsschott in 1951 in the Netherlands, the chubby-faced child, a boy who felt like a girl, broke loose of his parents' grip at the age of twelve to join the circus. By sixteen, Eva Maria Verba, her new name, had worked as a bellydancer on Hamburg's notorious Reeperbahn, stripped in nightclubs from Antwerp to Monte Carlo, and headlined at the Alcazar de Paris, known for its exuberant shows full of glam and glitter. Her stage name from then on was Romy Haag.

"As a transsexual back then, one had only two options," she writes in her autobiography, "to hustle or go into show business. I decided to do both. There wasn't anything else I could do." Haag was such a sensation—a rare beauty with talent—that an American show-biz agent booked her for a tour in the United States, where she performed for weeks on end in Atlantic City and on Fire Island. Photos from the day show a ravishing redhead with full lips and seductive smile posing in audacious outfits with plunging necklines and an array of see-through lingerie.

Friends tried to talk Haag out of setting up her own shop in West Berlin, convinced it would flop. Haag's vision was an extroverted, sexuality-celebrating burlesque show that fell somewhere between 1920s travesty and Andy Warhol's performance art. With $2,800 in startup capital, she rented a former disco in Schöneberg, which she did up in Art Deco style with black lacquer counters and plush red velvet curtains, crisply ironed white tablecloths spread on the tables. She recruited her international troupe from the bordellos and strip clubs across the city. Finally, she fastened onto the building's facade a high, eye-catching neon sign announcing, "Chez Romy Haag."

As it happened, West Berlin was ready for Romy, and much more. The very first night, all three shows—10 p.m., 1 a.m., 5 a.m.—sold out, and would remain sold out every night for months to come. The short acts, performed one after another in rapid-fire sequence, ranged from classic revue à la Mae West to star parodies, chorus lines, playbacks, and drag acts—all drenched in kitsch and camp. The last show, fueled by the evening's adrenaline and intoxicants, was usually the night's high point. Romy wore a slinky, glittering, full-length corset that in the spotlight lit her up like a disco ball. In the debut's encore, she dumbfounded everyone in the audience with an act that would become the club's signature. As she belted out the Welsh singer Shirley Bassey's "This Is My Life," she threw her earrings one at a time into the audience, ripped off her wig, and smeared lipstick all over her face. The crowd was speechless when the gig ended. What had just happened? they asked themselves. There was a hushed pause, and then thunderous applause.

Unwittingly, Haag ushered in a momentous transgender swerve that would play out in the city for decades to come. And, at the same time, she set off a veritable revolution in nightclub culture that doomed the likes of Christiane F.'s disco Sound. Haag's innovation, almost second nature today, was that she dismissed the pedestrian categories of "gay," "lesbian," and "straight" in exchange for a much broader, more nuanced category of "queer," even if she didn't employ the term that theorists such as Eve Sedwick and Judith Butler would popularize decades later.

According to queer theory—or likewise Haag's understanding of sexual and gender diversity—there are countless variations of sexuality beyond the dominant categories that society respects; sexual and gender identities are fluid, not fixed. It's not an exaggeration to say that this shift to "queerness," which Bowie had made years before, would transform the city like no other in Europe.

Chez Romy Haag was one of West Berlin's few late-night attractions that displayed some of the sparkle of the Golden Twenties. And, not coincidentally, by the time he arrived in Berlin, David Bowie was already a very close friend of Haag's. The two had met one night in West Berlin in April 1976, when Bowie was in town for a gig. Haag's club that evening was abuzz with the prospect of Bowie playing in the nearby Deutschlandhalle.

Romy Haag wasn't a big Bowie fan, even though one of the club's skits riffed off "Space Oddity" with the lines "Ground control to Major Tom / Take your hormone pills / And put your wig right on!" But Romy tagged along to the gig with twenty or so others from the club, populating the groupie-thick front row with dressed-to-the-nines transsexuals of every shape and size. The Deutschlandhalle was sold out, with Christiane Felscherinow and her stoner clique among the audience. "Everything was dazzlingly androgynous, and whoever knew how to use kohl eyeliner and lipstick did so with abandon," remembers Haag.

Thus the Haag coterie was a bit taken aback when Bowie stepped out of a wall of smoke in a bomber jacket, lit up by walls of fluorescent white light on either side of him. This traditional rock star getup wasn't what they'd expected. Nevertheless, the hall roared with approval. Halfway through "Station to Station" Bowie approached the edge of the stage, and leaned over toward the Chez Romy Haag crew. Romy flashed him a sensuous smile. "Suddenly our gazes met and fixed on each other—an intense experience that completely bowled me over, a kind of telepathic connection, and it was like I knew everything about this person," she claims to remember. "For a split second I forgot completely where I was and I had the feeling that we fell into each other's arms." She recollects: "It was clear to me then that something was going to come of it."

During the intermission, Bowie's staff approached Haag and said they'd like to come by the club after the show. Before the Chez Romy Haag troupe had even returned, the news of Bowie's pending visit had leaked out and the club was packed, journalists and camera crews thick on the doorstep. At the club, Bowie watched transfixed as Romy performed "My Life" and "Alabama Song" ("Show me the way to the next whisky bar"). The way Haag played with the ambiguities of sexuality and gender, as well as costumes and identity, was right up Bowie's alley.

After the show there was a little party back at Haag's penthouse for select guests. At dawn they began to depart until Bowie and Haag were alone. They kissed on the balcony and then fell into bed. But Bowie jumped up immediately and surveyed her enormous record collection. "Which David Bowie albums do you have?" he asked. "None," she replied, laughing. Bowie immediately phoned his people to have his complete discography sent over at once. The two spent the entire day together in bed, Bowie managing to get up and out the door to appear at his scheduled next gig in Hamburg three hours late.

Shortly thereafter, Bowie moved to Berlin. Days he spent at the studio, nights in her dressing room. At her place they'd turn off the phone and the doorbell, pull the curtains shut, and enjoy long afternoons together. Haag says that Bowie saw her as a mirror in which he saw his own androgynous self after the destructive period of Ziggy Stardust—the decadent rock-and-roll messiah—which he wanted desperately to shed. He and Iggy were regulars at the club, as was the filmmaker Fassbinder, among the many other celebs who passed through, including Grace Jones, Tina Turner, and Freddy Mercury. Bowie and Iggy were drinking copiously and, according to Haag, doing lots of cocaine, too. "You had to step over the two of them on the floor," she remembers. Still, it was like a rehab clinic compared to Los Angeles, Bowie's previous home.

Haag and Bowie accompanied West Berlin as a new era broke. One further manifestation of this was the café "Anderes Ufer" (Other Shore), conveniently located at 157 Hauptstrasse, two houses from Bowie's apartment. The café was the first of its type in all of Germany: an all-in-one coffee shop, gallery, restaurant, and night spot that beckoned to all homosexuals, transgender types, funky heteros, and anyone else who wanted to jettison the blinkered categories of the straight world. It marked the birth of uncloseted queer in West Berlin and signaled a new stage in the gay rights movement in Germany. Germany's first Christopher Street Day parade, now an annual international LGBT celebration and demonstration, would take place in West Berlin two years later in 1979.

While the lesbian and gay scenes had been cloistered in the past, Anderes Ufer boasted an unobstructed plate-glass window facing the street that let the light of day shine in. It declared, as if printed on the front page, that there was nothing that it or its patrons had to hide. In the summer you could enjoy your cheesecake and bowls of Milchkaffee at sidewalk tables. Anderes Ufer was like a shared living room for the Schöneberg crowd, including the regulars Bowie and Iggy, as well as rock star Nina Hagen, the publishers Heidi Paris and Peter Gente of Merve Press, photographer Nan Goldin, and cult film star Tabea Blumenschein.

Soon after opening, the café's owners, a male couple from Munich, found themselves in the line of fire, though not from straitlaced Schöneberg neighbors or right-wing thugs. A militant Marxist gay group griped that the café was "too commercial." The radicals smashed Anderes Ufer's windows late one night when Bowie was home in his apartment. He heard the commotion and hurried down to help out. The world-famous rock star kept watch over the shop for the rest of the night until the window could be repaired the next morning.

Musician Wolfgang Müller's first job in Berlin was at the café. "It was the only place where I could work where I didn't have to explain my sexuality," he says. "It was a place where many different types of people could meet. Take Blixa Bargeld, with his bizarre outfits. He didn't fit the classic male image. Or a woman like Gudrun Gut, who wanted to go out alone and not constantly be hit on."

In fact, Blixa Bargeld and Gudrun Gut—the nucleus of the first constellation of the band "Einstürzende Neubauten"—met each other at Anderes Ufer. Not long before the encounter, their names had been

Christian Emmerich and Gudrun Bredemann. The two weren't alone in taking on a nom de guerre, a deliberate act of wiping clean the slate, starting anew. "I thought for a dude with long hair, he has pretty good taste in music," Gut remembers the encounter with Bargeld.

Bowie departed a West Berlin in flux, and he left traces on it, as had Kommune I, the student movement, Christiane F., and Chez Romy Haag—all crucial impulses to the city's emerging underground pastiche. They contributed to a mystique of the western side of the divided city that seeped out to the rest of Europe and across its seas, too: Berlin, a place of extremes, a city in which to lose and then find yourself anew. A city with space to live and breathe and think.

By the time Bowie packed his last bag in Hauptstrasse in spring 1979, he'd already forwarded the rest of his things to a loft in Manhattan, his next port of call. Although nearly three years in one city was a comparatively long time for Bowie to stay put, it seems there was no one reason behind his leave-taking just then. The love affair with Romy Haag had cooled off during his absences: on world tour, vacation in Africa, acting stints.

In the meantime, Haag had become Germany's most illustrious and beloved transsexual, appearing regularly on West German TV. The two soul mates kept in touch for years—a postcard, periodically a phone call. Bowie told her he wanted to come back to Berlin. Though he visited for concerts, such as the storied 1987 gig alongside the Wall that sparked riots in East Berlin, he wouldn't stay for long. "Never again would I feel so free as I did in Berlin," he said many years later. One of the last songs that Bowie wrote before his death in January 2016 was "Where Are We Now?," a wistful look back at West Berlin.

Paul Hockenos, born in Boston in 1963, has lived in Berlin as a correspondent since 1989. He has written for The Nation, Foreign Policy, Foreign Affairs, The New York Times *and the digital* CNN. *He has authored several books on European politics and was a fellow at the American Academy in Berlin. His book* Berlin Calling *was published by The New Press in 2017.* *Photo: Hayyan al-Yousouf*

MARTIN-
GROPIUS-
BAU
200 m
ZEIT-
GEIST
INTERNATIONAL
KUNSTAUSSTELLU
BERLIN
'82

Willi and The Bang Chamber

By Ingo Lamberty

THE MAN IS wearing a black leather jacket and jeans, and his hair is definitely not orderly when he shows up at the telephone company in Berlin in February 1981 to register a phone. On the registration form he enters the address "Bülowstrasse 55, 1000 Berlin 30." Last name? First name? He considers briefly and writes "Schulz, Willi" on the prescribed lines. Willi Schulz is a longtime defender on the Hamburg SV soccer team. He played on the national team for a while and even wore the captain's armband a few times, but he always stood in the shadow of Uwe Seeler. Willi Schulz stands for doing one's duty. He is not known as a man of excess. No one asks for any identification from the man in the leather jacket.

And so, the squatted house in Schöneberg receives a telephone connection in March 1981 in the name of a rather boring but upstanding German national soccer player. Not unusual. Other squatted houses have telephone connections registered to names like Groucho Marx, and some don't get connections at all.

We were all looking for someone in West Berlin—me included. First, I searched the Journalism Institute at the Free University. Its reputation was legendary. Fritz Eberhard, a resistance fighter against the Nazis, was a professor there; also Ulrike Meinhof taught at the Institute who was a founding member of the RAF. Initially, I was a student in Mainz, first law, then journalism. The journalists teaching in Mainz, however, included Professor Elisabeth Noelle-Neumann, advisor to the Christian Democratic Union. I also had a problem with the Bundeswehr, because my status as a conscientious objector was not recognized. Politically, I was aligned with the Basisgruppen, grassroot radicals. So, West Berlin was the only option. During the winter semester in 1980–1981, I moved with two friends into a studio apartment with coal heating in Wedding. After that, I found an apartment in Neukölln, also one room with a kitchen, just for myself. And there I was: I didn't have to serve in the Bundeswehr, it was very cold in Berlin, and I was looking to connect.

There were a lot of journalism students in similar situations. They were new to Berlin and ready for anything. The Institute's current plan was to give up its locations in both the posh Grunewald at Roseneck and on Rüdesheimer Platz and to move to the former teacher training college in Lankwitz. We had never heard of that far-out part of the city. We saw the bad bus service—and went on strike. We printed fliers, painted banners, and finally occupied the Institute. A few of us in our first semester had already been to a squatters' demonstration. For some, it was their first rally ever. An article in the leftwing paper *taz* spoke of the "long-missing wind of freedom." Toward the end of the semester, when one of us said in the journalists' strike cafe, "We have to occupy a house," we had already had some practice. At least we thought so.

At the time, thousands of apartments in pre-war buildings stood empty, thousands were torn down each year, and tens of thousands of people were looking for a place to live. So, squatters had begun to occupy buildings for some years already. In 1980, the urban homesteading movement absolutely had exploded. New buildings were occupied almost daily. The police put up some resistance. On December 12, 1980, the squatted house at 48 Fraenkelufer in Kreuzberg was cleared. With the riots following the expulsion the West Berlin urban warfare began that left two hundred-seventy protesters and policemen wounded.

The squatting continued. About a hundred buildings were taken in the first few months of 1981 alone. The squatters had astonishingly positive popular support. Though the papers of the conservative Springer press, most notably, published reports of "radicals" and "stone-throwers," opinion polls showed that almost half of all Berliners accepted squatting in principle. The protesters of the 1970s had been peaceful hippies with long hair, but now, they wore their hair short and traded their flowing garments for black leather jackets. In the occupied buildings, the granola-muesli brigade met the molly brigade. There was a lot of talk about "war against the bloody system," not "peace and love." Legal, illegal, don't give a shit!

Our movement emerged not only to set ourselves apart from our parents, but also from the student movement of 1968 and its overly theoretical discussions. Though many of us were secretly in awe, some condemned them as driveling idiots. Similar ideas were common among young protestors in Amsterdam, Zürich, or London, where the Kraakers lived and Züri burned, while the Punks in London provided the soundtrack.

There were a few strong folks. Winnie, for example. He was a few years older than most of us and had been in Berlin a year longer, and he was also pretty handy. Jens seemed to know what he wanted and was a good speaker. Ulla was feisty and had something to say about everything. And Andrea just looked really good. I thought they were all pretty cool, though I never would've said so back then. And I wanted in. So, we moved into 55 Bülowstrasse, a dozen journalism students and a few friends we convinced on the fly.

The house was a giant complex near the Yorck bridges on the border of Schöneberg and Kreuzberg. Wim Wenders filmed a scene of his movie *Wings of Desire* (*Der Himmel über Berlin*) here, and a scene of *Cabaret* takes place in Yorckstrasse. The house had three courtyards and seven entrances. Several of them were already occupied by squatters, and we, the "Pubies," the students from the Institute of Publishing, got the first building in the backyard. It was still in decent shape, and we had paint brushes and screwdriver ready. Our goal was to occupy and renovate. We didn't want to destroy anything. Destroying was the policy of the Social Democrats; we wanted to repair the buildings. Our building belonged to the infamous Neue Heimat, a company owned by SPD-affiliated unions. They were part of the system. So, we were on the right side.

We established ourselves on one floor: a large communal kitchen, the Berlin Room for daily plenary assemblies, and two shared bedrooms. Winnie wore fine-rib underwear. Others sported psychedelic patterns from the seventies. We added a shower a few days later, followed by a room filled with mattresses for a little privacy: the "Fuck Room."

The most important thing was our daily meeting. Attendance was mandatory and we discussed everything: How we would renovate the building, the cooking and cleaning schedules, our conduct at demonstrations—stone-throwing or no stone-throwing, violence or no violence?

The topic of violence arose frequently. Except for two Berlin students from a Waldorf school, we were all children from the West German middle class. We came from Ingolstadt, Limburg on the Lahn, the Eifel, or the Westerwald, from Krefeld or Henstedt-Ulzburg, from

Bremervörde and Bargteheide. Our parents were teachers, architects, tradesmen, clerks, or businessmen. And most of us got along with our parents and called home regularly.

And suddenly we were talking about having to take on the cops. The pigs. Throwing stones, if necessary, some were saying. No way—that would bring us down to the level of the fascist system, others said. But what about caltrops? Can we use them? At some point we made some of those in the building's basement. Two large, bent nails, sharpened to a point at both ends, soldered together at the bends to form a tetrahedral. When the riot police drove a cop van over them, a Mercedes team-transport vehicle mostly, they busted the tires. Was that violence? Active or passive violence? We discussed that for an entire night. "Ultimately, we've got to learn to deliberately break laws that exist not to protect us but to protect the cops," one of the Pubies wrote. I didn't.

Of course, there were often arguments in 55 Bülowstrasse, as well as in the Squatters' Council, the informal high committee of the occupied buildings, about which direction the movement should be going in. The granola fraction wanted to secure their home with rental contracts. The mollies promoted a legal vacuum, revolution, anarchy, release of prisoners taken at the demonstrations. How boring that sounded: no demolition, self-determination for renovation, low rent. And we also definitely wanted to support the *taz* campaign, "Weapons for El Salvador"; we were united on that front. Because we wanted to be "Internationalistas." Why West Berlin, when we could be discussing El Salvador and Nicaragua?

Violence had its limits, however, as we learned when we discovered rats in the building. Many punks back then liked to walk around with white rats on their shoulders, to provoke a response. But a scruffy gray city rat was another story; those were disgusting. Winnie sprang into action: he caught one of the rats in a trap and set it on fire in the stairwell. The rat's death screams would drive the rest of the rodents away, he promised. It actually worked. The rats were gone, but an endless dispute broke out in the plenum, about whether rats should be treated so horribly.

I was a peripheral figure, right from the start. Not an opinion leader, like Winnie, Ulla, and the ultimate, Jens. Jens had a political career with the Communist League of West Germany (KBW) and an unsurpassed talent for agitation. Though I had my own flirtation with the

KBW under my belt, by that time I had already had enough of singing the "Internationale" around a campfire. Jens, however, liked to give fiery speeches about "communal working and living," which totally fascinated most of the inhabitants of Bülowstrasse.

My family history was to blame for my skepticism. My grandfather had already tried communal living and labor in the youth movement of

the 1920s and failed with his "new crop." My parents tried this again with a kind of rural commune in the Westerwald in the 1950s. So, I knew what it was like to share one toilet, when one gives speeches and the others rip the old wallpaper off the wall. And I liked to talk.

Incidentally, the Fuck Room was rarely used. While we were all the age of sexual maturity, we seldom made use of it. The appeal of the Pubies was apparently not sufficient enough to warrant withdrawing into the private room in pairs or more. Some made arrangements elsewhere, away from the building, which the hardcore faction didn't like. At the time, I was in love with Melanie. She was born in Ecuador, where her Jewish father had landed after fleeing the Nazis, and she was a student at the Institute for Latin American Studies. A revolutionary spirit had taken hold there, unlike that of any other university institution. Melanie was a member of the large group of allies supporting the squatters.

So far, everything should have been good. But the rest of the Pubies had two problems with Melanie. She looked great and wore stylish clothes, which had something to do with her job at an airline company. No holes in her jacket, no Palestinian scarf. And second, and this was the worst:

she lived in Friedenau, in bourgeois Friedenau! In a commune, but in a classy flat in an old building with central heating. And a bathtub!

It didn't matter that her community was taking care of troubled youth from the Märkisches Viertel. I had to defend myself at the plenum many times. The inquisition was in session: "Where were you last night?" "Why weren't you at the meeting yesterday?" "You're not participating actively enough!" "You and your barmy bourgeois bathtub relationship!" I did smell like pine bubble bath. Eventually, Inquisitor Ulla gave me a choice: Bülow or bathtub. She did not get her way. That time.

Now and then, however, our own ringleaders were put through the wringer. Winnie came from a wealthy family and owned two beautiful, old Art Nouveau apartment buildings in the best area in Cologne and lived very well from the proceeds. He tried to keep that a secret from us for a long time. When the truth came out, of course he was asked what he would do if one of his buildings were occupied by squatters. Was he now a part of the bloody system?

For some, our building was a free space wrested from the system. For others, it was a place of intense disputes about personal conduct. For all of us, it was the site of active political discussions. These disputes were driven with great zeal, at which we were rather adept. Almost all of us had been class or school representatives in our hometowns. And so, the kings and queens of the provinces came together and engaged in new battles to determine the top dog. That also meant that some of the former alpha animals had to realign themselves farther back in the Greek alphabet. As a result, some ringleaders became servants.

Seven entrances meant seven different groups at Bülow 55. We Pubies were the geeks in the building. There were groups that were better organized but did not stand out. Two groups, however, were something else.

On January 12, 1981, five gay men moved into the second building in the back of Bülowstrasse. That became the House of Queens, the first squatted house in Germany for gays only. The *Rosa Flieder* magazine reported on "fifteen to twenty gay lads, queens, sponties," most of them educationally privileged students who had just come out. The House of Queens quickly attracted gay visitors from West Germany, who saw it as a kind of youth hostel. Even there, solidarity decreased perceptibly, and all the original inhabitants had left before the eviction in winter 1983. The name "House of Queens" lived on, however; a housing project on Kastanienallee in Prenzlauer Berg still bears the name.

Our academic milieu had more trouble with the punks, who lived in the side wing of the third back building. They were the last group to arrive in the building and had to take whatever space was available. The punks were a fundamental part of the squatters' scene, certainly not the largest group, but the most conspicuous. They drank a lot, were not opposed to drugs, did not participate in political discussions in the building, and considered the concept of renovation to be "bourgeois bullshit."

We noticed that when they refused to steal coal from the Senate's reserve created during the Cold War in case of a new Berlin blockade. To do so, we had only to climb over a wall behind 55 Bülow, where the city of Berlin had set up giant coal supplies at Gleisdreieck, a triangular railway junction, if the Russians shut down the access points again. But the punks had no interest in climbing or hauling coal. So, they summarily burned a round of transoms and mullions from our beautiful wooden double windows, complete with paint and putty. Delegations from other groups tried many times to motivate the punks to steal coal, with no success. And yet Gleisdreieck, a space full of trees and abandoned rails was the best adventure playground ever in the middle of a big city. You could even climb into the bowl of the old water tower, which sported a white-painted squatters' symbol that was visible from far and wide.

The punks didn't care who came into or out of their building. If they even noticed at all. One day a Lebanese wholsale dealer established himself and supplied the small dealers on nearby Potsdamer Strasse with heroin and other substances. We thought that was incredibly stupid but we weren't in any position to inform the police. We didn't want the police to use a drug raid as an excuse to search or evacuate the building.

Long deliberations in various plenary sessions occured, then the solution: The next time the Lebanese man came to visit, all residents were called to the courtyard and formed a cordon. The bravest among us approached the dealer and said, "We're all looking at your face, and the next time you show up, we'll make you wish you hadn't!" After that, he had to pass through the cordon, and we all gave him our most vicious glares. He never showed up again.

But we loved the people from the Irren-Offensive, an anti-psychiatry movement. They were garrisoned in the squatted house next door, at 54 Bülow and were psychiatrically impaired, like Horst. Significantly older than we were, he was locked up as a spastic in an East German prison, until West Germany bought his freedom. He fought long to be able to be responsible for himself, and he was immensely proud when he got his first ID card. Horst never missed a rally. One day when he, a small, thin man with uncoordinated movements, was beaten up in a building entrance, most of the residents in our building became even more radicalized.

Squatting in buildings, unfortunately, was not a real full-time job in that it didn't generate income. For us, that was only a minor problem, as most of us were students. Each month we received money either from our parents or in the form of federal student aid. The cost of living in Berlin was much lower than it was in West Germany anyway, and we didn't have to pay rent, so we managed to make ends meet. Our academic studies weren't very difficult either, and leftist professors gave students "squatters' credits," for which we didn't have to do anything.

We really did learn a lot more in a short time in a squatted house, for instance about urban sanitation, police law, or psychology, than in some policy seminars at Free University.

Some of us still had to work, though, which was frowned upon in the building. If you weren't there, you couldn't paint a wall or clean up the kitchen. And we also figured out, sadly, that the workforce—the proletariat!—was not always sympathetic to the squatters. I had a job at *Der Tagesspiegel's* printing plant, from ten at night until three in the morning. The leftist, union-organized printers even took on sponsorship of one of the squatting houses. Still, there was talk each shift about "radicals, homos, and bums". And the talk wasn't friendly.

Same with the West Germans. Once, when I went to visit my friend Jan, who was the same age and had taken over his parents' farm in the Westerwald, I raved constantly to him about Berlin. I talked about the revolutionary atmosphere, the demonstrations, the sense of community. He listened for a while, rolled himself a Van Nelle cigarette, pulled his long hair into a ponytail, and left me sitting with the words, "I have to mow now." We were so full of ourselves.

Our parents, of course, were incredibly interested in us. Some even came to visit. When mine came to Berlin once, they were pretty anxious at first. But then they figured out that everything was neat and tidy, the toilet scrubbed, no mollies on the kitchen table. They invited me out to eat, and everything was OK. Claudia's father, a painter by trade, arrived with a truck full of paint cans, wallpaper rolls, and brushes. Nice kids. And a little bourgeois culture moved into the Bülow every now and then. We had a huge Christmas dinner, of course—before Christmas Eve, obviously, because we spent the holiday with our parents. Still, one of us lovingly drew a squatters' symbol on the gingerbread house. With frosting.

Once we organized a "Dinner from Home." Each of us was supposed to cook something from their region of origin. Of course, we all had particularly high expectations for Jim, from France. He tried to make crêpes. It is nearly impossible to make and serve crêpes for more than fifteen people all at once on a Berlin gas stove. The result? A huge batter-sludge disaster. Hannes from Ingolstadt wanted to serve Bavarian Weißwurst. But where could you get those in Berlin? In the gourmet section of the KaDeWe department store. The Weißwurst was delicious. However, discussions followed on whether squatters were allowed to shop at the über-capitalist, super-expensive KaDeWe.

Willi Schulz's telephone was in the front building, directly above the driveway, where the seven squat groups had set up a room for guards. The night watch was stationed there. In the event of an eviction, they were to set the telephone chain in motion, so in a short period of time, a decent crowd could be mobilized to protest. At least in theory.

Interestingly enough, the plan with the telephone worked really well. Generally, supportive living communities were called. And while three or four people set out for the demonstration, another one called the next on the list. “But why don’t the cops just disconnect the phone?” someone asked at a meeting. The answer was clear: “Because the line is bugged!” And suddenly the rumor spread that an ally, who had a student job in directory assistance at the telephone company in Winterfeldtstrasse, once took the wrong turn and saw a room in which the telephone numbers of all the squat houses were listed on a large board.

We liked using the telephone for hours for unnecessary conversations with just about anybody. For example, the question of whether we were allowed to buy the cheap “blue-band” margarine at a discounter or better margarine from somewhere else. Or we invented women (and men?) whose sexual attributes we discussed for hours. We had to entertain our friends in the intelligence service, after all, at least in theory. And so, Willi Schulz liked to make frequent calls, out of a combination of boredom, fun, and paranoia, about scabies, because the skin disease was spreading around the buildings, and we were all concerned. “Is it contagious?” Sometimes, however, we simply called our parents: “Hi, Mom, I’m fine!”

Willi Schulz was a well-behaved defender. And the Bülow was not a model house in the squatter scene, like the Kuckuck in Kreuzberg, whose giant fire wall sported an orange squatters’ arrow breaking through the upper right side of a circle, while three dark figures made a bomb below. Or the Kerngehäuse on Cuvrystrasse in SO 36, where many political initiatives were organized. Or the K.O.B. on near-by 157 Potsdamer Strasse, whose stage quickly became the performance site of hot bands.

The West Berlin government had been more or less firmly in the hands of the SPD hands for decades. In 1980, Dietrich Stobbe had followed Klaus Schütz as governing mayor and his SPD was responsible for the housing policy. Under the SPD, urban monsters were built, like the Neues Kreuzberger Zentrum at Kottbusser Tor, or projects at the edge of town, such as the Märkisches Viertel or Gropiusstadt. Redevelopment often meant gutting plus demolition of backyard buildings. That’s also what the Neue Heimat had planned for 55 Bülow.

In January 1981, however, Stobbe’s administration was over, wrecked by the usual West Berlin corruption and yet another construction scandal. The architect Dietrich Garski, member of the co-governing Free Democrats, swindled the Senate out of bonds of 124 million marks to finance the construction of Saudi military academies. For us squatters, this was new evidence of how rotten Berlin's policy really was. And the Social Democrats could not agree how to treat the squatters.

In May 1981, Richard von Weizsäcker of the CDU became the new governing mayor. The white-haired intellectual was beloved among the liberal middle class. He installed Heinrich Lummer as the senator of the interior. The avowed conservative announced a tough approach to take on squatters and other rebellious factions. At the same time, however, the left-wing Alternative List was voted into the House of Representatives, the first time for a party well-disposed toward the squatters.

The new CDU Senate tightened up the SPD's line. Not only would new occupations be prevented, but squatted houses would be evacuated. In September of 1981, Lummer announced measures against eight buildings, three on Winterfeldtstrasse and one at 89 Bülowstrasse. Many supporters moved in solidarity, but to no avail. The eviction occurred in the early afternoon, signaling the hour of Lummer's triumph. Accompanied by camera teams, he entered 89 Bülow, a building in rather damaged condition. While the senator was still smirking from the balcony, police brandishing batons drove about a thousand protesters away.

That was the moment when Klaus-Jürgen Rattay died. The 18-year-old jumped onto the bumper of the Line 48 double-decker bus, slipped, and fell under the wheels. On the death certificate, a policeman was said to have listed Rattay's occupation as "professional radical."

We were all shocked. In the following days, tens of thousands demonstrated, and barricades burned into the night. "Windows break, and you scream—People die, and you remain silent!" Rattay did not become a martyr, by the way; he was controversial even in the scene. He had run away from Kleve in North Rhein-Westphalia. After his death, an earlier interview he recorded with the TV broadcaster NDR aired, in which he said, "I just came to Berlin to take part in the squatter's movement and such. I retreated from society because I really didn't want to work anymore. Because we're continually oppressed at work, by a bunch of jerks. I've been here for one and a half months, and I like that there's such an incredible amount of toking here. I'm not afraid of the evacuations, but I also have the courage to fight." Because his fellow living companions didn't want to live with him anymore, he did not become a hero.

People like Rattay or the Punks of Bülow were the losers in the squatters' movement. They did not have a safety net, like us students. I had sublet my one-room apartment in Neukölln, just in case. Others had an shared space someplace else where they could crash when necessary. The kids on the run didn't have that, and we couldn't or wouldn't worry about them. We were busy renovating, studying, or being politically active. The Punks had beer cans for brains and no politics. Because of this, they had more run-ins with the police.

Back then, I often went to rallies with two friends. We called ourselves Alpha, Romeo, and Juliet, if I remember correctly, because Juliet's father owned a car dealership in Oldenburg. Alpha was a militant stone-thrower but looked like a bank clerk. He wore his hair short, and also a suit and a tie. "So I can walk past the cops without them asking for my ID." Once he was taken into custody, though, but was quickly released, thanks to a good lawyer. An estimated two-thirds of the squatters were students, and two-thirds of them came from West Germany. Like us Pubies.

Sometimes we just wanted to be cool. And then we didn't go to a demonstration, plenum, or the squatters' café. Instead, we went to the "Dschungel", a disco where we sat in the balcony, drank Barcadi Cola or cocktails, and convinced ourselves that we had seen David Bowie or Iggy Pop at the bar. At those times, Bülowstrasse was far away and New York really close, the only city that seemed on par with our West Berlin.

After Rattay's death, things were quieter in West Berlin. The squatters were busy sanding floors or discussing interpersonal problems. And elsewhere there were more important things than Berlin's housing policy. While hundreds of thousands were protesting NATO in Bonn, almost as many gathered in Brockdorf for the largest anti-nuclear rally to date in the history of the Federal Republic.

I lasted only half a year in Bülowstrasse, before I'd had enough of the Stalinists who liked to dictate when I could visit my girlfriend and what kind of job I could have. When one friend died of a tumor, there was no one in the Bülow house I could talk to about it, with one exception. And Martin, one of the Grand Inquisitors, declared in the plenum that he didn't think much of "bourgeois grief." I moved into Melanie's room at the commune in Friedenau, though she had broken up with me in the meantime. I kept going to rallies or the squatters' cafés, usually freshly bathed. I no longer gave any thought to scabies, though.

The Pubies stuck it out in varying configurations. Some followed after me, lacking the energy to stay. Others lacked the energy to leave.

Soon the group was divided. There were the "ringleaders," whose kitchen was called the "head kitchen." And there were the "non-adults," with the "softy kitchen." Sometimes one of the ringleaders went to the "non-adults," simply needing to rest for a while. Over time, the Pubies organized themselves like in the large communes. The rooms were renovated. More and more furniture came into the house; beds replaced mattresses on the floor.

The Bülow house was active one more time. In 1982, when U.S.-President Ronald Reagan came to Berlin, the "Lappenkrieg", the "rag war" was raging. Everywhere, not just on squatted houses, banners were hung: "Reagan eff off." The one on our façade read, "The president is stupid." The district attorney's office got involved, citing paragraph 103 of the criminal code: "Defamation of agents of foreign nations." A clever attorney made it clear that it had nothing to do with Ronald Reagan, but with the president of Hertha BSC. He was not an agent of a foreign nation, nor did he file any defamation complaint. Thus, the matter was closed.

When 55 Bülowstrasse, one of the last squatted houses, was cleared in late 1983, nearly one hundred people were taken into custody. Hardly any of the original crew of Pubies were still there. The house went the way of the movement: resignation, fragmentation, dissolution into factions. The sponsors and the allies alike had long since retreated. The energy fizzled, in the end. The stalwarts took off in the face of impending eviction and now lived more middle-class, in an apartment or a shared space. Those taken into custody hardly had any perspective. Only a few were sentenced. Trespassing was the most frequent offence, followed by theft of electricity. But the judiciary got tangled up in too many ludicrous secondary offences, like having sex near an open window.

In 1984, the last of the squatted houses in Schöneberg's Mansteinstrasse was given rental contracts. Of over 160 squatted buildings, sixty were ultimately evacuated, and others were legalized. Many were simply given up. A few years later, I happened to move with my roommates into a formerly squatted house on Goebenstrasse, practically in sight of Bülowstrasse. The landlord, still the Neue Heimat, treated us decently, and nothing in the building called to mind its former status. Only Schimala's thrift store on the ground floor had survived unchanged.

The last hardcore squatters remained in Kreuzberg SO 36, where there's a clash with the police every year on May 1. Initially, radicals from the squatters' scene initiated in the May riot, but lately, primarily Turkish and Arabic kids are the ones working out their frustrations.

We middle-class kids from 55 Bülow have mostly turned our backs on Berlin. We're living in the Eifel again, or in Bargteheide. We've moved to Bremen, Cologne, or Königswinter. Two of us ended up in California. We became editors, professors, city planners, teachers, or real estate owners. Some of us have died, and others do not want to be reminded of their time as squatters at all, because their current friends, the ones in the Rotary Club, wouldn't understand.

Twenty-five years later, some of us got together, and old wounds and unrequited loves resurfaced immediately. Even beforehand, when we were coordinating via email, we accused each other of being "gutless opportunists" and "egoists." And then there were the ones who still felt compelled to explain how the world works, because they've been able to "keenly study the processes." The ringleaders and those who still haven't figured it out. Hardly any of the 2nd-class squatters came to the gathering.

Politically, we had no clear mission, which distinguished us from the rebels of the sixtiess. Some were looking for fun or adventure. We did achieve one thing: We put an end to large-scale building demolition of Berlin's pre-war buildings. And—the irony of history—the apartments we maintained and renovated are now inhabited by people earning good money, in Kreuzberg, Charlottenburg, and Schöneberg.

One question, however, will forever remain unanswered: Did anyone ever pay Willi Schulz's telephone bill? And if so, who? Not the former soccer player, in any case. He's now an insurance agent living in Hamburg.

Ingo Lamberty, born 1959, grew up in a water mill in the Westerwald and studied in Mainz and Berlin. From 1985, he reported illegally from the GDR for the taz. *In 1989 he became a reporter at* Tagesspiegel, *where he received the prestigious Theodor Wolff Prize. Since 1992 he has worked in TV, first at* VOX, *then at* WDR *for* Morgenmagazin. *He is married with one son and lives in Cologne. Photo: private*

Survival in Berlin

By Rosa von Praunheim

BERLIN... CITY OF Lost Souls: that is the title of my 1983 film, the story of several American singers and dancers who were stranded in Berlin and whose biographies inspired me to improvise a feature film about their lives. Many of them are already dead. Tara was murdered in Tiergarten Park. Beautiful Tron died of AIDS, Angie Stardust of cancer, and talented Black dancer Gary seems to have disappeared.

Only Lorraine, punk singer Jayne County ("Man Enough to Be a Woman"), drag star Joaquim la Habana, and the versatile Judith Flex are known to be still alive. Now the film has been rediscovered internationally because it's a historical display of Berlin before 1989, when the Wall was still standing: an island of outsiders where creative people from all over the world met. Rents were cheap, the nightlife endless, and the gay scene was unique in Europe.

I came to Berlin in the early sixties to escape military service. I studied free-style painting at the Academy of Arts and lived in a storefront apartment with other artist friends. The police long suspected that we were running a narcotics ring and watched us from a flower store across the street. On my 21st birthday, there was a raid. At the time I was painting murdered kings, and there was a Punch puppet hanging out of one of the paintings. I'd hidden marijuana in it, and the cops didn't find it.

For a short time, an architecture student lived with us who wanted to turn me in when he found out I was having gay sex. He wouldn't even use our bathroom anymore. The anti-gay Paragraph 175 of the criminal code, taken directly from Nazi law, still existed at that time. If charges had actually been filed, a court would have had to convict me.

From 1949 to 1969, twice as many gay men were convicted in West Berlin and West Germany as during the Nazi era; the only difference was they landed in prison instead of a concentration camp. Finally, in

1969, the Paragraph was liberalized in favor of gays, although it wasn't completely abolished until 1994 in united Germany.

In the sixties, I had caused a sensation with my short films that also dealt with homosexuality. Bavarian Television asked me on behalf of WDR, the biggest German public TV station, if I wanted to make a feature-length film about homosexuality. I did so with pleasure. I shot the film very subversively without synchronized sound, but with a very provocative voice-over. This is how my sensational, scandalous film *Not the Homosexual is Perverse, but the Situation in Which He Lives* was made in 1970.

In that film, I let out all my rage at the cowardly gay scene in West Berlin. Most gays, as I had experienced it over many years, were apolitical and uninterested in their own emancipation; they preferred to take refuge in glamour and movie-star fantasies. They entered gay bars furtively, had sex in dark parks, and were always in danger of being beaten up by homophobes in public toilets. It was hard to meet politically like-minded people. And the leftist groups were as anti-gay as they were anti-woman. When the movie premiered in 1971, it caused furious indignation; but a small minority of gays took it as an opportunity to form the first gay liberation groups.

Television banned the film, so we showed it in cinemas, never without heated discussions, by the way. During this time, over fifty gay groups were founded. Finally, in 1973, the film made it on television and became a big hit. Gays in East Berlin could also see it, and gay activists over there founded the first liberation group. Unfortunately, the group was soon forbidden by State Security, the all-powerful secret police.

Berlin was the liberation for me, too. I grew up in Praunheim, a district of Frankfurt am Main. I was very sheltered and shy; only in Berlin did I dare to live out my gayness. But in the circle of my artist friends, there seemed to be no gays. I was considered eccentric and wild, and I expressed that in my paintings and poems. 1968 was the time of politicization. Many students were protesting against authority and also against the Vietnam War. Most of them considered art to be reactionary at that time, because leftist ideology saw art as nothing but a means of propaganda. I didn't like mass movements. At that time, I only participated on the fringes of the many rallies on the Kurfürstendamm, West Berlin's main boulevard, because I saw myself as an individual. Even later, when many of the political firebrands turned to drugs or joined sects, I didn't participate. Nevertheless, I attracted attention at film festivals. With my cult film *The Bed Sausage* from 1970, I got really big publicity. For the movie, I brought my elderly aunt Luzi together with a hustler from West Berlin, and we parodied a heterosexual love affair. To this day, the film is loved by young people. So I quickly became famous.

But my following films flopped. That's why I went to New York, where I shot successful documentaries, among them *Survival in New York*, a movie about three young German women in New York; Ulrike Buschbacher, Claudia Steinberg, and Anna Steegmann (as pictured above in a New York subway car). That enabled me to continue working.

The eighties were marked by the disease AIDS, to which many friends in America and Berlin fell victim. For almost a decade I devoted myself to prevention work with films, talk show appearances, and newspaper articles. It was an emotionally difficult time. Many of my friends didn't want to lose the sexual freedoms we had fought for so laboriously, and they downplayed the peril of HIV and AIDS. At the time, however, there was no viable way to ameliorate it. The disease meant dying in agony.

This also changed Berlin. But that was only the beginning. When the Wall came down in 1989 and many gays from the East came to the sexually liberal West, they were fascinated by the sex clubs and sexual freedoms. But I was very afraid that this could mean a death sentence for many. My strident safer-sex campaigns became more and more furious. In 1985, I made one of the first films on AIDS: *A Virus Knows No Morals*. It was a deliberate black comedy meant to educate with humor. When we showed the film, there were good discussions, but we also experienced protests and ignorance. I remember disputes with young, handsome gay men who didn't take our warnings seriously or even mocked them. Many of them soon became tragic victims of the virus.

It wasn't until the mid-nineties, when new drugs curbed the danger of AIDS, that the gay scene became more relaxed again. Today, Berlin is once again the capital of sex and wild nightlife. Meanwhile, there is Prep, which is supposed to protect against HIV infections, but of course not against STDs like syphilis and gonorrhea, or against hepatitis. The young gay scene has become more careless and numbs itself with drugs.

Yes, Berlin is getting expensive, rents are rising and apartments are hard to find; but the city is still a magnet for artists and outsiders from all over the world. I've now made over one hundred fifty films, many of them with gay themes. Last year I made a movie about Berlin's new creative center: *Survival in Neukölln* shows the international diversity of the artistic and gay scenes there, centering on the wonderful Juwelia, who has been running a small club in the south-central district of Neukölln for many years and enchants her guests with her charm.

In the meantime, I have become old. In November 2023 I will celebrate my 81th birthday. I have been fortunate to live in a wonderful relationship for eleven years, and I am finally enjoying the quiet side of Berlin. I will remain faithful to this city. This is where I will die, and until then I am enjoying the diversity of a great, wonderful city. The success of right-wing parties makes us aware that we should not take our democratic freedoms for granted, and that we must always remain vigilant and active.

Rosa von Praunheim, director, author, and winner of many film awards, is considered an important representative of the post-modern German film scene and a pioneer of the gay and lesbian movement. In over fifty years he has made more than one hundred fifty movies. Born Holger Mischwitzky in 1942 in Riga, Latvia, he grew up in Frankfurt/Main and has lived in Berlin since the sixties. *Photo: Markus Tiarks*

S
Anhalter Bahnhof

The Ghost Train

From The Südost-Express

ONE DAY, AFTER many years of animosity, West Berlin experienced its first rally in favor of the S-Bahn, as opposed to against it. On January 8, 1984, the commuter train with its trademark red-and-yellow cars would finally be "liberated from Communist reign", the *Berliner Morgenpost* wrote triumphantly. The West Berlin transit authority, the BVG, was poised to take over the West Berlin routes of the city-wide S-Bahn that had previously been under the management of the Reichsbahn, controlled by East Germany since the partition of the city after World War II.

The days after the takeover would be the busiest for a long time. Thousands of West Berliners took the S-Bahn to Heiligensee, Frohnau, or Lichterfelde Süd for the last time before the lines were shut down by the BVG for the time being. Refurbishment was urgently needed. The cars were exceptionally full that last day, the tunnel walls only dimly lit by the illuminations. Strangers reminisced about the good old days, their memories of the underground. All of these passengers were saying goodbye—temporarily—to a mode of transportation that had once been among the most modern in Europe. And they could not wait to say "Hello" again.

Since the Wall's construction in 1961, the S-Bahn had been badmouthed. Riding it was politically incorrect in West Berlin. That was because the S-Bahn was operating under the management of the East German Reichsbahn, at the behest of the victorious Allies of World War II. So if a West Berliner were to buy a ticket, even if it was dirt cheap, he would be showing support to the enemy in the East. Only a few days after the Wall was built, Willy Brandt, then-mayor of the Western half-city, called for the first boycott of the S-Bahn, so the German Democratic Republic—the GDR—would not get "Western money for buying barbed wire."

It didn't matter that the North-South line of the S-Bahn provided the fastest connection from Anhalter Bahnhof to Gesundbrunnen. The obedient West Berliner took the bus despite an hour-long detour. The pinnacle of the battle for the S-Bahn was the railroad gate in Tegel. When West Berliners had to wait there, they did so with much displeasure, counting the commuters on the passing train: "We are stuck here because of ten people," they liked to grumble.

The North-South line, built from 1934 to 1939, is the only significant structure within the S-Bahn grid that is underground. It was destroyed in the last days of World War II, when the SS blew up the tunnel below the Landwehrkanal. More than one hundred people drowned, since the

S-Bahn cars parked down there served as emergency hospitals. It wasn't until two years later that the trains started rolling again. When the Wall was built, the S-Bahn stations from Potsdamer Platz to Nordbahnhof were locked, bolted and walled up, with the exception of the Friedrichstrasse border crossing, which remained heavily guarded. When the North-South line passed the City center - part of East Berlin—its trains would pass through ghost stations, where GDR border patrol stood guard and nobody could leave or enter.

Ghost tunnels are by no means unusual in Berlin. Schöneberg, for instance, has several ghost tunnels for the planned Subway line 10, below Kleistpark, Innsbrucker Platz, Schlossstrasse and Rathaus Steglitz. But when the S-Bahn was taken over in 1984 by the West, it included a line to the Wannsee that ran parallel to the future Subway line 10. Hence, the U10 was abandoned. These are subway structures owned by the BVG and therefore on record in the West.

There are also two subway lines, No 6 and No 8, that pass below the East Berlin city center. Their stops became ghost stations as well, where trains run slowly and tourists get spooked. Berlin also has lesser-known ghost stations, with no trains at all. These are located in the Western part of the city, secret and completely hidden. A few weeks ago, the Süd-Ost-Express set out to find them, a long and ambitious research trip into the city's underground.

This story begins a few days after the aforementioned January 8, 1984, when the S-Bahn made its first tentative comeback in West Berlin. The place we sought out was Anhalter Bahnhof, an underground S-Bahn station in Kreuzberg. Here, the northbound train enters the long north-south tunnel that crosses right under East Berlin, all the way up to Gesundbrunnen. The attentive straphanger will probably wonder about a second platform, a platform without tracks. It leads into a tunnel, but after a few feet, this glimpse is blocked by a wall.

Ours was blocked as well, and so we continued our research in a nearby pub. The barkeeper told us that the trackless platform was the beginning of an already finished tunnel to Görlitzer Bahnhof a few miles east, below Oranienstrasse and passing the Moritzplatz subway station. "There are lots of tunnels leading to all kinds of places," he said. "I haven't scouted everything out yet. But I can go underground right here in the pub and get to the other side of the street." Unfortunately, he went on, "the entrance was closed because of rats." A patron in the bar told us about hidden platforms behind the ones we'd seen at Anhalter Bahnhof. We would be able to recognize them from the missing tiles on the wall. That happens, he said, because of temperature differences between the part of the station in use and the disused bricked-up shafts behind the walls.

We reckoned that there was some truth in that. As early as 1938, while the North-South tunnel was still in construction, several additions had been planned, including one line that would have branched off from Potsdamer Platz and led to the never-built Great Hall of the People north of the Reichstag. And that underground line from Anhalter Bahnhof to Görlitzer Bahnhof was also conceived at this time, writes Peter Bley in his book Berliner S-Bahn. It was supposed to be the East-West Underground. However, only a short branch from Anhalter Bahnhof was actually completed; the neglected fourth platform edge we saw at this station bears witness. A green door at the end of the dead platform allows access—if you have a key.

However, while most of those ideas didn't get past the planning stage, there was one part that had actually been constructed. This is the Moritzplatz S-Bahn station, completed as early as 1926 and built during the excavation of the Subway line 8. It is located directly under the Moritzplatz subway station, oriented from East to West. It is in shell state only, with raw concrete stairs and track beds without tracks. During the war, it was used as an air raid shelter. But there may be more. In our next endeavor, we talked to former Reichsbahn employees who had been in charge of the city registrar office. They assured the Süd-Ost-Express that they had seen older blueprints of the S-Bahn grid. According to those old blueprints, an underground S-Bahn station Görlitzer Bahnhof already exists. But is has been kept secret to this day.

This S-Bahn tunnel below Görlitzer Bahnhof—so they told us—is thirty to fifty feet below ground. It was dug, excavated and braced from 1939 to 1942 by foreign forced laborers and inmates from a nearby concentration camp. During World War II, it was used as an ammunition factory and as a weapons storage facility. But it was actually intended to be part of the S-Bahn at Görlitzer Bahnhof. Plans existed to extend it all the way to Königs Wusterhausen far South.

According to those former employees of the Reichsbahn, the Building Department in West Berlin should have had corresponding plans. However, inquiries within the Building Department did not yield any results—we only heard speculations that an ammunition bunker may or may not exist somewhere in the vicinity of Görlitzer Bahnhof. In addition, several older Kreuzberg residents living in the area told us about bunkers that were supposed to reach to the so-called "piss tube," the pedestrian tunnel under the station grounds.

The idea that the construction of the S-Bahn was tied to secret strategic planning during the Third Reich is not unreasonable. In 1968, the *Morgenpost* wrote of "sensational discoveries": the City's Office of Bridge Construction detected large and mysterious cavities below the Tiergarten. "A fifteen feet deep 'lake' discovered—old tunnels below Tiergarten," was the *Morgenpost* headline of June 11, 1968. And on December 1, 1968: "Was the Soviet monument built on a tunnel crossing? Old drawing confirms tunnel system in Tiergarten." The article continued: "As we reported yesterday, the SS and the Organisation Todt—a subgroup of the SS—had set up a heavily guarded secret storage facility for weapons, rations and

files in one of those tunnels ... The SS weapons magazine was quite obviously located in this S-Bahn tunnel."

Of course, we spoke to the editor in charge at *Die Morgenpost*, but he had long since thrown away his notes. There was, however, an informant (this at least he remembered), a former Wehrmacht soldier who had given him a drawing of the tunnel system. Sadly, that was also gone. At this moment, we could only assume that some kind of an underground connection existed, but we didn't know any details. Coincidentally, the Office of Water Management then commissioned drill holes within the Görlitzer Bahnhof, in preparation for a new park. But so far, they have not unearthed any evidence for the existence of a secret station. These drillings—which will be thirty feet deep—were only done to find oil-contaminated soils, not old ammunition, the office told us.

However, the Süd-Ost-Express never gives up. A few days later, we reached out to the Allied occupation forces—who are not particularly known for their openness—but sadly, that didn't get us anywhere either. The American officer in charge of Kreuzberg was ill at the time and not available for information. The vague assumption of the West Berlin Building Department that an underground bunker may exist below Görlitzer Bahnhof had apparently not prompted the Americans to conduct their own research—or at least not to make it public.

Then again, it would be really irksome if the proposed park at Görlitzer Bahnhof were finished—and all of a sudden traces of old ammunition bunkers would appear. In the south of Tempelhof, a park had been built on former train terrain only recently, and the land had been dug up beforehand in search of ammunition, something that had happened on the basis of far flimsier evidence. And not that long ago, a kindergarten in Methfesselstrasse had to shut down because the Borough office had found out that it was built on top of an old ammunition chute. Perhaps the Berlin City government still remembers the house in Buckow that blew up last month because a few bombs were stored only twenty inches below the basement. So, why not dig here?

We paid our next visit to Günter Hecht, the media spokesman of the BVG. Hecht had at least heard of the mysterious station under Görlitzer Park and he knew of the proposed tunnels from Anhalter Bahnhof. "The tracks were supposed to spread out to the southeast, in the direction of Görlitzer Bahnhof", he told us. The question was, however, "to establish who is the landlord," he explained. "It's tremendously complicated: the S-Bahn doesn't belong to the GDR, bear in mind, the S-Bahn belongs to the German Reich, and the German Reich, which no longer exists, is still formally there, though now administered by the Allies." That sounds like madness, but that's actually how it was. And the GDR, Hecht continued, could not exercise any sovereign rights for the S-Bahn, it only had operating rights. "So, in plain German, they are only running it, not owning..."

But how far S-Bahn tunnels were driven and whether air-raid shelters were built was beyond the knowledge of the BVG spokesman. Hecht didn't know what was "planned during that time and what really exists," especially given the fact that the Reichsbahn folks "took everything with them that was tangible. The even ripped solid objects from the walls" during the 1984 handover.

The old plans are located at the Reichsbahn Construction Office in East Berlin, he said. The BVG would only want to access them if needed for a construction project. Before we left, Hecht promised us that we would be allowed to see the secret Moritzplatz S-Bahn station—which was supposedly partly under water—and even bring cameras along. Unfortunately, however, he withdrew that offer sometime later—too much water in the secret shell, he said. The water level in the shell could not have been the reason that we were not allowed to go underground, though, because only a few years earlier American troops had been playing Civil War down in the tunnels.

But we were not completely out of luck. A few days and a fair number of persistent phone calls later, the bureaucrats at the BVG allowed us to step through the green door at Anhalter Bahnhof that we had encountered in the beginning, and to finally get a glimpse of the sealed tunnel

- accompanied by a security guard, of course. On the day of the appointment, however, no one at station management knew anything about the promise made to us. Hours passed. Only the intervention of the initially skeptical, but soon friendly manager of the station prompted two gentlemen from the BVG headquarters to finally show up at the platform. The key to the door had disappeared and only much later reappeared, they explained, justifying the delay.

At that point, we had already had been told by a worker that the tunnel was only three hundred feet long. After those three hundred feet, a wall would close the shaft. Our informant could not tell us whether this wall had been built in 1961, which we assumed, or whether it was older. But he knew that the tunnel had been built by forced laborers as well. They had been housed in an adjacent catacomb. The underground track was mostly finished—only the gravel and the rails to let the trains roll were missing. The construction looked sturdy and it seemed unlikely that the wall marked the actual end of the tunnel. On a rise, the tunnel may well continue beyond the walled line.

But as far as the hidden tunnels under the Görlitzer Bahnhof were concerned, the search for certainty remained unsuccessful. We were left with rumors and dark suspicions of tunnels between East and West, inklings of escape routes and catacombs, haunting memories of the labyrinth of sewers we know from the movie The Third Man, set in Vienna.

To get entirely to the bottom of the S-Bahn-story, we reached out to our readers. A few of them told us similar tales of white crocodiles that are said to vegetate in the tunnels and sewers of Berlin, ever since they or their ancestors, brought from faraway lands to grow up here, were flushed down the toilet by their worldly owners out of respect for the voracious reptiles ["This story is getting weirder and weirder;" *comment of the typesetter*]. The flushings were also in response to traditionally cramped living conditions in West Berlin that don't allow for large pets.

The hints and rumors and assumptions we gained from our readership allow us the postscript "and if the crocodiles are not dead, they lived happily ever after." ["So always close the toilet lid!"; *the typesetter*]. However, as interesting as this is, we would prefer to get more information on the hidden S-Bahn tunnels and ghost stations for our next issue. Please call.

The Südost-Express was published from 1977 to 1990 in the urban renewal area of the most Eastern part of Kreuzberg. At its peak, the magazine had more than thirty volunteer editors, reporters and photographers. The Südost-Express was devoted to topics such as urban development, squatting, civil disobedience and police brutality. The magazine also wrote about street festivals and Kreuzberg history.

Wannsee Beach

By Harald Martenstein

The Strandbad Wannsee, Wannsee Beach, is supposedly the largest landlocked beach resort in Europe; that's how it's been described in Berlin travel guides for ages. It is large enough to accommodate the entire population of a small town and it has a corresponding number of beach chairs. It was also the inspiration for the most famous beach hit in German history, "Pack die Badehose ein," i.e. Pack the bathing suit, by Conny Froboess. Language critics might suggest the word "perspiration", instead of inspiration, because a beach is usually hot.

In late summer, the Strandbad Wannsee has an algae problem. At this time of year, it stinks, at least a little bit. But if you stuff both of your nostrils thoroughly with two tissues, then even in late summer you might think you're somewhere near the ocean, especially if you've had a bit to drink beforehand, and you probably should have anyway.

During the summer, Strandbad Wannsee is the main social meeting place for the two most important social groups in the city, namely the West Berlin proletariat and the West Berlin subproletariat. These two groups have been rivals for moral supremacy in the city since anyone can remember. They dislike each other, and Wannsee is their preferred place for their quarrels.

The proletarian can afford a beach chair, thanks to one hundred years of SPD-rule and trade unions. They drink cocktails or fancy guava juice at the beach bar, they wear bling in their lobes or in their belly buttons, and they feel God knows how important. But in reality, they are a dying class. They forfeited cultural supremacy a long time ago, for they have become flabby and self-absorbed. The proletarian men expand their waists substantially in their early thirties. At the same age, the proletarian women have their breasts enlarged.

The subproletarian simply looks better. The subproletarian man goes to the gym for six hours every day instead of going to work, so he still has a sixpack at age sixty. The chest of the subproletarian woman is well-trained, brown as cocoa, and heavily oiled. When she walks, her breasts drip and make a rhythmic noise, kind of a luscious kapsch-quatsch. If that happens, the proletarian man stares at the subproletarian woman, he just can't help it, and he gets into trouble with his wife.

The proletarians think that money can buy everything. But you can't buy beauty with money, at most you can put work into getting it.

The subproletarian sits on a towel and listens to "Modern Talking" on a radio the size of a washing machine. Subproletarians drink beer, because if you do a lot of sports you can afford it, figure-wise. All subproletarians sport elaborate tattoos, even in places where you never would have guessed, or wanted to guess. Some have brought tattoo trade magazines along to discuss the latest trends regarding tattoos in many special terms. Lately, the tattoos mostly display Far Eastern motifs, they are riffing off Yin and Yang and Zen and Dragon Ball and the multi-layered philosophies of the East. This is because the subproletarian travels a lot and is interested in foreign cultures, provided they get tattooed.

In addition, there are three other social groups in the Strandbad Wannsee, namely the Turks, the gays and the parents of small children. These three groups don't really have issues with each other because they wisely stay out of each other's way. The gays used to meet on a specific terrace to hook up, but this building was closed a long time ago because it was about to collapse. Most of the Strandbad's structures suffer from acute danger of collapse as well as from rapid crumbling and being overgrown by huge plants. The terrace has been decaying for decades. Every year, it looks more and more like the bunkers of the former Westwall on the French Atlantic coast, half-sunken in the sand.

And yet, the Strandbad Wannsee has been under constant renovation since 1983. It is the longest redevelopment work that has been carried out on a public bath on the entire planet, ever. Even the restoration of the ancient Roman baths of Pompeii went faster, despite them being in a lousy condition, due to that infamous volcano. How long ago was the year 1983? It was the year when Ronald Reagan ruled the United States. In the Soviet Union, Yuri Andropov had just succeeded Brezhnev. Björn Borg had ended his tennis career, and also the T.V. series M.A.S.H. went off air. Many people learned about a new disease called AIDS for the first time. In Bonn, thousands rallied against Reagan's Star Wars program that included new medium-range nuclear missiles in Germany. And in East Berlin, the state leadership inaugurated the faithfully rebuilt French Cathedral at Gendarmenmarkt, or, as it was called at this time, Place of the Academy, which took six years to construct.

Strandbad Wannsee is a generational project, comparable to the relocation of the temple of Abu Simbel in Egypt, which was still completed faster, in four years. The redevelopment of the Strandbad was already in the planning stage when Klaus Schütz was mayor of West Berlin.

During the short reign of Hans-Jochen Vogel, the project seems to have been put on hold. The actual construction work began when Richard von Weizsäcker was mayor. And Eberhard Diepgen and Walter Momper seem to have worked tirelessly throughout their whole time in office on rebuilding the showers, repairing the toilets and finding a restaurant leaseholder. However, there is still as much work to be done as before.

The subproletarians like the decay. They say, "This place looks like Level 3 of Dragonball Destroyer." The proletarians, however, keep writing letters of complaint to their district councilman.

Since the gays no longer have their terrace, they mingle with the subproletarians. The two groups are not easy to distinguish because they both have a high degree of muscle build-up due to constant gym-training. The most useful rule of thumb is: a man who has more intimate zone piercings than tattoos is probably gay. A man who has more tattoos than intimate zone piercings is probably a heterosexual subproletarian.

It is almost impossible to drown in the Wannsee. For the water to be deep enough for you to drown, you first have to wade two or three miles into the lake on the shallow end of the beach. That's why Wannsee has already saved many lives. For many a world-worn man has changed his mind on the long walk, while wading past a beautiful woman on the way to the depths, or a smiling freshwater guru from India, or even past a headhunter who offers him a wonderful job. Finally, he thinks, "Oh, life is not so bad after all," turns around and sends a letter of resignation to the Association of Suicidal People.

For the same reason—because of its shallowness—the parents of small children also love Wannsee. Only when the parents want to teach the children to swim, does it get difficult. The children simply can't make their way into the depths with their little legs. They stay near the shore, and when they are ten, they can't swim, but they know everything about piercings and tattoos.

Turkish Berliners have also made their way to Wannsee. I recently encountered an older Turkish woman entering the beach with a headscarf and a body-lenght outfit. She sat under a parasol; laboriously, she took off her shoes and her socks and watched for hours what was happening at the beach. Her husband ran right over to the nudist section without much hesitation. There, he also sat under a parasol and watched the women while he tirelessly let his little pearl strings slip through his fingers. Eventually, he went back to his wife and ate a snack she had prepared in the meantime. Afterwards, he strolled back to the nudist beach.

Around 8 p.m. the bath empties out. The proletarians scold the subproletarians because they are leaving their garbage behind. Occasionally a subproletarian leaves with a proletarian woman he has conquered, but never a proletarian with a subproletarian woman. Everyone goes home. But there is still much to be done.

Harald Martenstein, born in 1953, is the author of the "Martenstein" column in ZEITmagazin and also an editor at the Berlin daily Die Welt. *In 2004, he received the Egon Erwin Kisch Prize. In addition to his award-winning novel* Heimweg, *several of his collections of columns have appeared as a book, including* Männer sind wie Pfirsiche *and* Jeder lügt so gut er kann. *Photo: C. Bertelsmann Verlag*

Architects and Tanks

By Mary Pepchinski

In the summer of 1987, I left New York City and headed to West Berlin. My life in the Big Apple had become unbearable. The ever-rising costs of living in New York City made it necessary that I—a young single woman, who desired to make her mark in architecture—labored not only in a large architecture office but also took on freelance projects to pay for a hopelessly overpriced apartment and finance my inventive furniture and art installations. Although I had exhibited these objects in galleries to acclaim, after five grueling years, I was ready for a change.

Two years previously, I had visited West Berlin for the first time during an extended trip to the Netherlands and West Germany. The Europeans I met impressed me with their decidedly more relaxed lifestyle: they only worked one job, took vacations, and they had the time to enjoy a long dinner or a Sunday morning grappa with hours of good conversation. Everyone's rent was cheap. I desperately wanted this existence. Looking back, I could have gone almost anywhere, but West Berlin won because there was much international attention being lavished on the ambitious International Building Exhibition, the IBA, that was taking place in these years; friends were waiting for me there, too.

As I purchased a train ticket to West Berlin from some town in West Germany I can no longer remember, I was surprised to learn from the ticket seller at the Deutsche Bahn that the journey would take seven long hours. At the time, my grasp of European geography was still shaky. I had assumed that Berlin was some sort of appendage attached to the German-German border.

Once I examined a map, the absurdity of the city's situation sunk in. My parents were equally out-of-touch when I informed them about my decision to spend some time in West Berlin. This was surprising, because both had served in the American Army during and after World

War II in Germany. Whereas I was ignorant, they had first-hand knowledge, but it was frozen in time. Perhaps remembering the ravaged cities or the Berlin airlift of the years 1948-49, my father inquired anxiously: "Do you get enough food to eat?"

My mother had been a sergeant in the Women's Army Corps with the occupying forces in Berlin-Zehlendorf in 1945. She had been working for a colonel who was collecting evidence for the Nuremberg Trails, a task that left her deeply unsettled for the rest of her life. But she seemed oblivious to the effect of the Berlin Wall.

When I returned home for a visit, she mentioned that their office had been on Unter den Linden. "Do you go there often?" she wanted to know. "Yes," I answered, somewhat facetiously. From time to time, I did make my way to this grand boulevard that extends eastwards from the Brandenburg Gate. But it was too exhausting to explain that it was segregated off in East Berlin, or to worry her with the knowledge that Americans were now persona non grata in this part of town.

As I adjusted to West Berlin, I grappled with a city that felt in equal doses familiar and strange, like Freud's definition of *unheimlich,* uncanny. My idea of a modern city had been formed by Manhattan's soaring skyscrapers, bordered by spectacularly wide, deep rivers and connected to the mainland by towering bridges, whose nests of cables held up high, arching roadways. With this image fixed in my mind, I expected all contemporary cities to live up to this ideal. If this is downtown, where are the towers? Could this trickle possibly be the Spree river?

Devoid of high rises and a muscular waterway, there were, nonetheless, aspects of West Berlin that reminded me of New York. Both were islands, and one was conscious that to enter or leave required an extra dose of planning, as only a few access points—bridges and tunnels in the one case, military checkpoints in the other—were available. Once on the island of one's choice, it was possible to spend months, years, or even decades there, with all one's needs met, from recreation to work, entertainment and consumption, in a landscape that varied from rough thoroughfares to tree-lined neighborhoods and generous, leafy parks.

And both also had a gritty side. Beyond the sparkle and buzz of Midtown Manhattan, New York in the 1980s was comprised of many low-scale neighborhoods, like the Lower East Side and Harlem, and even more so numerous parts of Brooklyn, the Bronx, and Queens. Small shops lined the streets, where a similar mix of people—students and artists, working and middle class, some local, others from all over the world—went about their lives. In West Berlin, I was drawn to similar neighborhoods, like Klausener Platz in Charlottenburg, the area around Winterfeldt Market and Goltzstrasse in Schöneberg, and the Landwehr Canal from Hallesches Tor to Schlesisches Tor at the easternmost parts of Kreuzberg at the Wall.

I traveled there via subways that were—in my New York opinion—relatively clean, efficient, and not terribly loud. Upon arrival I wandered around or spent time in a café: the granularity and grime felt comforting. But some of West Berlin's antiquated ways were hard to fathom. A city of two million inhabitants whose shops closed between Saturday afternoon and Monday morning seemed absurd, even if this was the law in all of Germany. What was I to do on a Sunday morning if there was no milk for my coffee? Wait until the grocery store opened on Monday?

Asking the neighbors somehow never occurred to me, and I cannot remember anyway meeting any of the tenants who assiduously kept to themselves in that post-war apartment block near Kurfürstendamm in the district of Wilmersdorf where I first lived. The handful of after-hours shops, like Ullrich's at Bahnhof Zoo, where I could buy milk, packaged white bread, powdered soup, and a generous assortment of schnapps, were never an appealing alternative. I preferred to wait until a nearby café opened and grab a cappuccino.

The unfriendliness and provincialism of the West Berliners was another disappointment. Shopkeepers would grimace as if in pain, when I attempted to speak their native language. One of them told me auf Deutsch: "German is a difficult language. Only the Germans can speak German correctly!" I was coming from New York, where it seemed like every other person was foreign born and spoke accented, often ungrammatical, English. Such a mean-spirited response deeply contradicted my understanding of how a world city (and I assumed that West Berlin aspired to be one), and its citizens, should be. It also made me feel that I was not welcome in this hopelessly outdated place.

Momentous events in New York soon upended my plans. Walking down Kurfürstendamm in late October 1987, I came upon kiosks displaying copies of the *International Herald Tribune*, whose banner headlines announced the crash of the New York stock market. One third of its value had been lost in a day's trading, and tough economic times were ahead. Although I was planning to return home, I knew that employment, especially as an architect, would now be hard to find there. While in West Berlin, I had been surviving on a mix of short-term jobs and my modest savings, but this was hardly a long-term strategy.

Fortunately a friend who was a teaching assistant at the architecture faculty of the Technical University Berlin proposed me for teaching contract. The job was intended for a foreign architect. I clinched the position due to my New York experience, combined with a design award I got and positive reviews of my inventive furniture and art installations in publications from the *New York Times* to *Andy Warhol's Interview*. Thus, my career in academia was launched, and by the fall of 1988 I received a regular, extended contract as a teaching assistant.

The architecture faculty occupied an eight-story, glass and concrete slab overlooking the vast traffic circle at Ernst-Reuter-Platz in Charlottenburg. There were roughly fifteen professorial chairs, upwards of forty teaching assistants and over one thousand students who all appeared to operate according to the principle of supervised anarchy. The professors could relegate their duties to the teaching assistants, such as myself, and then occupy themselves with other tasks for weeks. But although I had to follow the themes I was contracted to teach, I had a great deal of freedom. And so did the students. At times they would even dictate to me when they planned to show up for instruction or what topics they intended to pursue. Somehow the system functioned, and learning took place.

While the faculty and its denizens could seem suspended in time, the building's immediate environs were firmly rooted in the brutal present. At least twice, I left the building and saw a seemingly never-ending column of American tanks barreling down Bismarckstrasse, snaking around the traffic island at Ernst-Reuter-Platz and speeding down the Strasse des 17. Juni to the Brandenburg Gate and the Berlin Wall. It was impossible to cross the street while this manic demonstration was taking place, and I remained captive in the architecture faculty until it was over. I had never experienced anything so terrifying. Closing my eyes, the effect was like relentless hordes of stampeding elephants, whose rumble echoed about the streets and the flanking buildings, while the fierce rhythmic pounding of their caterpillar tracks literally shook the ground.

Previously, I had enjoyed years of studying for a master's degree at the architecture school of Columbia University in New York. In contrast to the brutally competitive world of practice, that institution, housed in an intimate, finely detailed, neo-classical building, and filled with students and faculty passionately wrestling over the merits of one design or another, was a pampered refuge that I dearly relished. The atmosphere

at the architecture faculty of the Technical University, known as the "TU", was a letdown, in comparison. The capacious building felt like a place that we passed through, but never really inhabited. The hallways were poorly illuminated and uninviting, devoid of the lively clutter that advertised lectures and displayed projects and publications. Strict hierarchies were enforced to distinguish the teaching assistants from the tenured professors, and the latter usually rebuffed my greetings when we shared an elevator or passed in the hallways.

As I started to work at my desk in a shared office, I discovered fading reports about Marxist-Leninism stashed away in a drawer, relics from the bitter protests of the Sixties. The carefully typed pages recounted the theory of the working class and its oppression. And the thinking was still virulent. Once, I prepared a teaching exercise to analyze modern villas by famous 20th century architects like Ludwig Mies van der Rohe, Le Corbusier, and Alvar Aalto. A student assistant harshly called

me out for propagating a bourgeois housing type, which would soon become obsolete because the revolution would happen any time soon.

In the fall of October 1988, I noticed there was something amiss after we had completed our first exercise, a small housing and construction design. The students had become unusually reticent and were reluctant to discuss our next task. I have no idea how much they knew in advance, but suddenly and without warning the building sprung to life. Giant sheets, painted in bold colors and declaring "Strike!" and "Solidarity with Wessiland!"—West Berlin slang for West Germany—hung in the high, light-filled entrance lobby and the façade of the faculty.

Following their peers at the other universities in West Berlin and much of West Germany, the architecture students were going on strike.

Higher education in West Germany is tuition free, a notable distinction to the United States, where I had taken out hefty school loans to finance my studies. So German students had the luxury to extend their time at university for as long as they felt necessary or join a prolonged action—like a strike. I marveled at the freedom these students enjoyed because they were unburdened by material pressures. But as I soon learned, the strike had economic roots. By the 1980s, rising numbers

of students had led to overfilled lecture halls and staff shortages. There were also funding cuts, and strike organizers claimed this was done to direct resources to areas of greater benefit to industry and commerce.

When the strike was announced, the architecture professors, who were anticipating a semester without students to instruct, handed over whatever duties were left to the teaching assistants, like me. My fellow teaching assistants however, who looked forward to a semester with less workload, immediately expressed support for the striking students. Simultaneously, they retreated to their fledgling architecture offices. I had the suspicion that this was not the first time that a strike had taken place.

A new word, or rather a new abbreviation, entered my German vocabulary: the "VV" or Vollversammlung—general meeting—, where everyone gathers to discuss a pressing matter. The students held their "VVs" in the Audimax, or main auditorium, to express their grievances. In addition to calling for adjustments to enable them to finish a degree in the proscribed time, they demanded more inspired and relevant teaching.

I assume the tenured professors held their own "VVs" too, but they were probably squirreled away behind closed doors. Meanwhile, the forty or so teaching assistants, ranging in age from their mid-twenties to late thirties, met in some institute or one of the building's two cavernous atriums for our own monthly "VV." We discussed how we should respond to the directives from the administration. It was not only exciting to sit in a big circle and meet colleagues who were starting to win architecture competitions, build, or write books, but also to experience the faculty being gently resuscitated after decades of deep sleep.

Although I did not see masses of students in the building, they were around. At other faculties in West Berlin they were more visible, and students took over the teaching and created their own "autonomous" seminars. Sometimes their actions spilled onto the streets. They marched through downtown West Berlin to the city hall in Schöneberg, where John F. Kennedy had spoken, and held sit-ins and events on subway platforms to keep the West Berliners informed about their grievances. The architects contributed to these actions too, like coming together en masse, with protest signs ablaze, on the traffic island in Ernst Reuter Platz, to communicate their demands to rush-hour commuters.

For the most part, the architecture students were using their time-out to fundraise, collecting small donations from the hundreds of their striking cohorts to fund a three-day long, very well-attended symposium called "Teaching Architecture." Held in early February 1989 in the Audimax of the architecture faculty, "Teaching Architecture" commenced each day in the late afternoon and extended well into the evening. Escaping the chilling temperatures and the biting dampness of a Berlin winter for a spot at this event, I was happy to find myself among the unexpected comfort and warmth of an impassioned group of like-minded individuals. The interior of the Audimax felt dim and murky, but warm spotlights cast a golden glow, like a campfire in a clearing, around the speakers and panelists assembled on stage. Hundreds of attendees sat in the steeply rising rows of seats, reveling in the intellectual nourishment they received from this spectacle.

The students invited an impressive collection of local and even a few international speakers, who discussed themes like "Project-oriented coursework after 1968," "Teaching Architectural Design," "Bauhaus and today," and "Experimental Building." My bachelor's degree was from a women's college in New York where my classmates and I had lobbied the administration to establish a major in architecture. So, I, too, was invited to join a panel about "Feminist Approaches for Architectural Education." One of the invited speakers was a member of the Matrix collective in London, a group of women architects who applied for public funding to develop socially oriented projects for immigrants.

She showed slides of the group at work and told stories about how they involved the future users in the design process. This included an outdoor "brick party," organized for a community of Pakistani women and their children to help select the material for new family health center. That the users, often with modest education and means, were treated with respect, and their opinion was highly valued, was an epiphany for me. My American education had portrayed the architect as a lonely genius who creates brilliant, artistic designs, not a humble person who makes buildings for those who are marginalized and takes their input seriously. Listening to such talks, my professional horizon was expanding, too. To accompany the symposium, the organizers also compiled an one-hundred-page photocopied booklet, which I have kept to this day.

By the spring, passions had dissipated, and we all returned to the classroom. Life in West Berlin may not always have been pleasant, but compared to my existence in New York, it was never boring.

Born in 1955 in Yonkers, NY, Mary Pepchinski studied at Columbia University and worked as an architect in New York. In 1987, she relocated to West Berlin. Now retired, she was a professor in Dresden and held guest professorships in Mainz and Graz, Austria. She publishes widely about architecture. In 2017, she was an advisor to the "Frau Architekt" exhibit at DAM in Frankfurt/Main. Photo: private

Foundling Bird

By Gerd Nowakowski

This story is based on a series of articles that appeared in the daily paper taz *in summer 1988 about a bird that fell from his nest into the kitchen of the editor. They are based on a true story (mostly).*

Down and Out – When the Weather Plays Fate

IT IS NOT a pigeon. I wouldn't have allowed THAT bird into my house. I think it's a young crow— or maybe a raven? A shocked bird perched in the gutter between the cars, letting its stubby wings hang. Next to his—or her?—nest, shattered, thrown on the ground by the downpour from the branches high above.

Quite large, the creature. Gray feathers, still a little fluffy, a large, dark beak, not quite as pointed as a crow's beak, rather quite bulging. The two-legged thing looks well fed and strong, but is obviously not fit to fly yet.

What to do? Leave it for the dogs to eat? No. Getting it away from the street and into the green backyard is also no solution, because that's where the fat orange tomcat is lurking. Let's take it home. I'll put it in a box. The beast pecks and flaps its wings; it seems a bit nervous.

"And what next?", asks Volker H., my flatmate.

No idea.

The debate is taken to the newsroom of the Metro section, which is where I work. "You need to feed it worms, of course," Tillack the environmental reporter says.

"Water and bread," young man Malzahn grumbles in his usual young-man-confidence.

"Put it on your shoulder and teach it to talk," Caroline, the intern, chimes in. She did not take into account that the critter has already shat all over the box and filled it in one night only. If I put this bird on my shoulder, it will only learn to swear, if anything.

This is clearly a case for an expert.

So I call the zoo. But no luck: "We can't connect your call to the bird house," the receptionist says curtly. "Ask a pet shop."

I choose the pet shop Hannibal, since it has an elephant in its logo. There is a lengthy period of speechlessness. Then they suggest calling a veterinarian.

Instead, I call "Rex-the-Animal-friend", the Neukölln branch of a pet store chain. They actually enlighten me with their feeding suggestions: insects and maggots, grains and also a boiled egg, no need to peel it, the friendly lady says. How does she know? She just raised a sparrow that had fallen out of its nest. I am convinced.

But I'm already anticipating the next problem. Assuming the bird doesn't croak, how do I teach it to fly?

Please call: *taz* survival helpline, Metro editorial office: 4609-246

gn

***

First Strikes. Help! How to Feed a Beast?

Foundling Bird is being difficult. He already had to be rescued twice, because his flights—or escape attempts—ended ten feet below in the green backyard and the fat orange tomcat was on the scene immediately. So we had to catch him again and put him in the box.

He shits all over the box and also all over the kitchen with frightening speed. If we give him something to eat, he croaks wildly from his downy throat and pecks everything in the vicinity of his first-strike weapon like a little devil.

One mystery has been solved, however. Foundling Bird is a hooded crow. This is the result of an inspection by friends who count themselves among the knowledgeable, as well as telephone calls from *taz* readers.

However, there are protests from the readership against yesterday's nutrition tips from the bird experts. Crows are carnivores, says Helge F.. Based on his own experiences in bird raising, he recommends minced meat. Rolled into small balls and stuffed in the bird's mouth, they bring concentrated energy. Mrs. B., who has already raised two crows, recommends cottage cheese. When the crow gets older, dog or cat food. After all, the crow is a nest predator that preys on dumps and is also an omnivore. Like the expert from Rex-the-Animalfriend she too recommends a hard-boiled egg—but without the shell. Eggshell is too hard for a young

bird. If we want to feed it calcium, it's better to buy it at a pet store, so the beak can become truly hard.

No way! It is already hard enough, as I have had to learn. Because all those feeding suggestions have one downside: the beast does not play along. As Mrs. B. says simply: If he doesn't want to eat, hold his head and open his beak. And if he pecks, just slap him. Easier said than done. Since even gloves are useless, the food is now presented on the tip of the dustpan, with my fingers outside the beak's reach.

How advisors can suggest feeding the Foundling Bird with tweezers is beyond me. Before we can use the tweezers, we have to get the bird under control. And how would we do that? Throw a blanket over the bird to wrap it into a straitjacket? Or huddle up on the little shitter like a football team?

Good advice and/or encouragement please urgently to *taz* survival helpline, phone: 4609-246

gn

***

Under Control: Foundling Bird is Force-fed

Count to three, grasp decisively, and Foundling Bird is firmly in the headlock - only the head is still free. Then we have to press the bulging beak open with one finger of the left hand, while the fingers of the right hand are used to press the good ground beef into the gullet; just in small portions, as if they were little worms.

Foundling Bird, named after the Grimm's fairy tale of the same name, squirms and fights off his supposed enemy—me—with all the malice of his young life. But at least he swallows what is drilled into him, whereas on the days before he hadn't even looked at the hard-boiled egg. The substitute bird parent—me—is satisfied.

What about drinking? How about injecting water down the throat with a disposable syringe? Nonsense, says roommate H., they don't get any water in the nest either. He says this in a firm voice—just like men do when they have no idea.

I remain suspicious. So from now on, force-feeding. Only the prospect of grabbing the beast three times a day turns me off. Because when he's released, he pecks me again. Does he hate us, even though roommate H. threw one of our good ashtrays out of the window to rescue him, because the fat orange tomcat had climbed the window sill of the ground floor apartment again? Foundling Bird should just be grateful, shouldn't he?

gn

***

Mucho Macho: Foundling Bird Puffs Himself Up

Foundling Bird is becoming a party animal. He waved goodbye to the jaded fatalism he radiated in the first days after falling out of his nest. Force-feeding has also become unnecessary; he still pecks at the food-

giving hand, but much more tenderly than before. In addition to the good ground beef, he has also discovered the tasty orange as a dispenser of liquid. For he still refuses water. Not a drop enters his beak despite the gagging efforts of two grown men.
In company, Foundling Bird comes out of his shell. As soon as people are talking near him, he wants to be there, spreads his wings, stretches and makes himself bigger than he actually is. Or he puffs himself up until his head almost disappears in the mass of feathers. Do the men in our shared apartment encourage him to behave in this way?

Now *taz* author Eva S., driven to the apartment by maternal instinct and the worst suspicions about animal cruelty, shows up: "He'll pull through. Pigeons are tough, you know." Foundling Bird is not a pigeon. Eva is banned from the house in the future.

gn

***

It Stinks! Foundling Bird is a Stinker

Foundling Bird—presented in this paper as a young crow for several days —is a young pigeon. So claims our photographer Erik Ouwerkerk, who is also a biologist. The difference: the crow has a thick, heavy beak, Foundling Bird on the other hand has a long, thin beak. Is Erik right? I don't think so.

Foundling Bird stinks. Not only does he shit incessantly, but the longer he's in the house, the more his smell can't be ignored. Now I understand why Mrs. B., who had a hooded crow for six years, spoke tenderly and ambiguously of the "flying wild boar".

What to do? In the first days, the concern for Foundling Bird's survival was so paramount that the smell was accepted. Now, however, roommate Härtig is wrinkling his nose. Maybe he is infested with vermin? Who knows. Shall we bathe him? Then again; after his traumatic experience with the thunderstorm that knocked his little nest off the tree onto the street, along with himself, we want to spare him another shock. A vermin spray is needed; the nozzle is aimed at the feathers and squeezed off. Foundling bird flaps its wings. He is not at all interested in whether the stuff is supposedly completely harmless.

In the end, the plumage hangs down dripping, and instead of a ball of feathers, a gauntly fluttering bird presents itself until the sun dries him up again. But: he still stinks.

gn

***

No Pigeon! What Have I Done to Deserve this!

I'm crushed. Did I bring a disgusting pigeon into my kitchen with Foundling Bird after all? "It is not a pigeon. Because a pigeon would not have been allowed into my house", I declared in this very newspaper last Thursday. And two days later, once again breathing a sigh of relief, self-confirming: "Foundling Bird is a hooded crow. This is the result of an inspection by friends who presumably know." Pah, false friends.

What happened? Photographer/biologist Erik Ouwerkerk is adamant that Foundling Bird is a pigeon. Summoned to the surrogate nest—our shared kitchen— he stands firm. He pulls out his identification book, brought from the Netherlands, and points to a pigeon. "That's him," he says. After all, he once scientifically observed otters as a biologist on the Shetland Islands, and he also spent six months raising a crow.

"But the beak, long, wide and bulging, no pigeon has that," I protest, pointing out the window at the flying nasties in front of our house.

"That will change with time," Erik insists coolly, and his consolation does nothing for me: it is the somewhat rarer wood pigeon, though also a long-time native to the city.

So I fatten up the enemy in my kitchen, with the good ground beef and lots of love, have it peck at me and clean up its shit every day—I can't effing believe it. What is the legend of Oedipus compared to this drama [No worries, I know a good therapist! *The typesetter*]?

What to do? Shall I tip the rearing box in front of the greedy snout of the fat orange tomcat immediately? Have we barred the tomcat from attacking, just to be disappointed like this? Shall I keep nourishing Foundling Bird until he's fledged, but with constant resentment in my heart, until he joins the army of the cooing bastards?

taz readers help! Awaiting advice at 4609-246.

gn

***

Foundling Bird Go Home!
A Berliner Can't Be Seen With a Pigeon

Our relationship is disturbed. Foundling Bird has lost all amiability and is ornery. He is right. Only with reluctance he receives his food, since it is clear that Foundling Bird, who has fallen from the nest, is not a hooded crow but a pigeon. After revealing its true nature, Foundling Bird immediately received another disinfection shower.

As a native Berliner, you can only hate a pigeon. With a pigeon in the house you are threatened by social isolation. The "rats of the air" are not only disgusting disease carriers, they always cross you on a bike, court reporter Plutonia comments, also a Berliner. She treats me as if I have committed high treason.

"Abominable, abominable," chokes out colleague Brigitte Fehrle: "I could poison them all myself," she adds. Even Metro editor Thomas Rogalla, who hails from the Ruhrgebiet, only says "uh" when asked about his relationship with pigeons. Given the thousands of pigeon breeders in the Ruhr, he sees pigeons as the symbol of "petty bourgeoisy".

Only editor Elisa Klapheck praises the "aesthetic" birds, with the "beautiful gray color, whose shape has a certain swing" [And thus almost the entire Metro editorial staff would then have proven themselves to be racists... besides, I just remember: Isn't the dove a peace symbol? *The typesetter*]. So before any social acceptance in the social environment is lost by the further possession of such a stupid bird, Foundling Bird must go.

The handover over to the fat orange tomcat, however, is rejected for reasons of conscience. Driving to Wessiland on the weekend and "losing" the bird on the transit route? Too cumbersome.

My best bet is an ad: Young pigeon for sale,
Offers at 4609-246,
gn

***

Foundling Bird is Gone.
Enough With the Crow That Was a Pigeon

Mr. Wonderous is seventy, has a large white beard, is a little like his name and has an incredible knowledge of birds. He is a member of the German Association for the Protection of Birds and probably an honorary bird.

His wife is also seventy, and also a bird expert. Both live in an apartment whose walls are filled with shelves of bird books. Every free spot is filled with pictures of birds, but all really fancy ones, like vultures, ostriches and condors.

When I enter the apartment, with Foundling Bird in the cardboard box, his wife just says, "Oh, a plain domestic pigeon, I can hear that right away."

Mr. Wonderous doesn't hear the high notes so well anymore, otherwise he would have said that right away too, he remarks. Well fed, he says. I nod; all that good ground beef. But now, he says, there's an end to fattening up a pigeon that was supposed to be a hooded crow that had fallen out of the nest. That's why I'm there. Because I don't want to raise the unmasked pigeon any longer.

Yesterday evening I was tempted to leave the bird in the trash can. It had ended up there involuntarily after an attempt to fly: it landed on the swinging lid, the lid gave way, the bird plopped into the trash can, the swinging lid swung back again. Foundling Bird was caught.

But I couldn't bring myself to leave it in the can. That's why I visited Mr. and Mrs. Wonderous. They will now escort him on his way to freedom. Then the flying rat will shit all over everything. I just hope it doesn't hit me.

gn

***

Addendum (and an Almost-Happy Ending)

Mr. Wonderous calls me after I finished the above post. He said he bathed the pigeon and after extensive cleaning determined that it was an almost fledged wood pigeon and not a common domestic pigeon, which is a feral rock pigeon. The wood pigeon is the largest wild pigeon in Europe, much larger than the nasty domestic pigeons, Mr. Wonderous knows. Only a minority of them stay for the winter in Berlin, most of them move to warmer regions. I'm glad about that. And the probability that the pigeon will poop on my head in the future has also decreased.

gn

Squatting in No Man's Land

By Martina Schrey

My foot. He simply grabbed my foot. At the same time, he looked at me from below with wide eyes and kept talking to me, or rather, at me. It wasn't just about urban planning or the protection of nature. It was about challenging authority. Finding out how freely we can, and want, to live. To see how far we could go. But he just wouldn't let go. I always have this moment in mind when I think back to July 1, 1988.

The story began five weeks earlier. I had just started as a young reporter in West Berlin and on that sunny day on May, I covered a rally for the left-wing alternative Radio 100, the first private radio station in West Berlin. Organized as a grassroots democratic radio and chronically underfunded, it had been on the air for more than a year at that point. We worked at the radio out of conviction— there was no money to be made. The rally marked the first anniversary of the call for boycott of the Federal Census. A year ago, an alliance of activists had called for resistance against the "surveillance state" and against data mining that was seen as overblown.

The participants marched through the Tiergarten and past the Lenné Triangle, a triangle-shaped piece of land named after the famous landscape architect Peter Joseph Lenné. Ten acres of wild green, located the West side of the Wall, but legally belonging to East Berlin—and, until recently, cordoned off by a narrow steel fence. For the last month, however, some unusual action had been going on. East Berlin construction crews had removed the fence and had created access roads for trucks.

But today everything was quiet. The Lenné Triangle was only a few hundred yards from Potsdamer Platz. Only now and then a car drove along Entlastungstrasse, a four-line road with no name. Butterflies sailed in the wind and birds chirped, while leaflets were handed out. I took one too and stuffed it in my pocket without looking at it; it was already late. I wanted to go to the Radio 100 station for my daily broadcast.

Only two days later I realized what had happened. About thirty people had crossed the inner-city border the night after the rally and had occupied the Lenné Triangle. A site once located in the heart of pre-war Berlin, opposite the former luxury hotel Esplanade at Potsdamer Platz. Now it was no man's land, sunk into a sleeping-beauty-like slumber. Since the construction of the Wall twenty-eight years ago, no one had set foot on that piece of soil. Birch trees and brush grew on the former Lennéstrasse, which had been a fancy residential address between Tiergarten and Potsdamer Platz before World War II.

This area was to become the property of West Berlin on July 1, 1988, as part of a larger exchange of territory. But the West Berlin city government had by no means paid the price of seventy-six million Marks to grow potatoes or plant kale. A big chunk of the land was earmarked for the six-lane expressway that would finalize the Autobahn around West Berlin's city center. But, as of today, the triangle still belonged to the GDR.

The flyer was still in my pocket—and sure enough, it was an appeal to protect the plant and animal life that had "already fallen victim to human civilization" elsewhere. More than one hundred and sixty species, some of them threatened with extinction, were at home here, the flyer continued. The Lenné Triangle was not a wasteland, but a "wild, undeveloped urban paradise" that needed to be protected: "If you are up for summer, life, laughter and quarrels, then please come here so that we can keep the place!"

And just like that, I made my way to the squatters. By now, they were least fifty people. They told me that at first, the GDR border guards had asked them to leave, but after some consideration, they were allowed to stay. The squatters wasted no time in setting up the first tents. "Riot—Resistance—This is our land" was written on a banner with a black star, the symbol for the autonomous, left-wing movement West Berlin was famous for. Black and red flags were waving in the wind. Without further ado, the area was renamed to Norbert-Kubat-Dreieck, after a young man who had taken his own life in detention after a riot on May 1st in Kreuzberg.

A community tent was set up, organized by a left-wing collective from Kreuzberg, and next to it lay the so-called Volxküche, a communal kitchen. The Alternative Liste, the West Berlin forerunner of the Green Party, had also settled someplace. The left-wing activists got their water from the permanent legal campers at Potsdamer Platz, the "Rollheimers": people in circus wagons, old wagons and buses. And a restroom was not far away either, as there was a Porta Potty for the tourists at Potsdamer Platz.

As a reporter of Radio 100, a medium that was very close to the left-wing-alternative movement, it was easy for me engage with the squatters. I looked around: While the squatters were busily working away, they were being watched with great interest from all around. The tourists who came here in droves to take a shuddering look at

the dreariness of Berlin's Mitte, to get memorabilia at the souvenir stalls on Potsdamer Platz, and to catch a glimpse of the East across the Wall from a platform—they were delighted about the additional spectacle. "Caution, beware of squatters; photography forbidden, feeding allowed," read a poster on a wall covered with notes and post-its. The squatters had put it up to protect their ever-growing village of tents and huts. And many out-of-towners benevolently left a few marks or dollars after being led along the "Ho Chi Minh Trail" between the settlement. They rejoiced at this oh-so-crazy-Berlin-experience.

Of course, more and more journalists arrived, first from the Berlin media, but soon also nationwide and even foreign press. The East German border guards behind the Wall also never tired of pulling out their cameras to document what was happening. They had handed over responsibility to the West Berlin police, who would have to ensure that the "territory of the GDR" was cleared. But that was impossible for the Western guardians of the law, since due to the Allied occupation status, they were not allowed to enter the area. Accordingly, they remained

standing, their toes right behind the demarcation line, never taking their eyes off the action on the grounds.

Even the Allied occupation forces could not do anything: The part of the city surrounding the triangle was British territory. They were allowed to enter the eastern sector and thus the Lenné Triangle, but they were not allowed to exercise sovereign rights. And so, for the time being, the squatters were allowed to do as they pleased.

The senator of the Interior in West Berlin, Wilhelm Kewenig, a conservative Christian Democrat, was anything but relaxed. He warned that the Lenné Triangle still harbored ammunition from World War II. But the squatters ignored the danger. Kewenig, however, was not deterred. Under the pretense that he wanted to prevent further influx of squatters for their own protection, he had the just-removed fence around the triangle rebuilt after only two weeks. This made access more difficult—but not impossible. The Wall did not run exactly along the borderline in this area. A narrow strip on the West side still belonged to the GDR and was thus off-limits to the Berlin Senate. The police were helpless and the squatters still could get supplies.

The first garden plots were laid out; goats and chickens also found a new home on the triangle. The birch trees cleared by the construction workers from the East served as building material for more solid huts that withstood the weather better than the tents. In the meantime, the squatters founded their own radio, *Radio Zanzibar,* which undauntedly broadcast everything it thought was newsworthy. And it had two press spokesmen: Stephan Noé from the Alternative Liste, who kept the press at large up to date, but preferred to retire to his Charlottenburg apartment to sleep. In addition, "Info-Stefan" reported to the reporters who lived on the premises. They in turn provided insider information, especially to left-alternative media representatives like me.

The most important question was: What free spaces exist in West Berlin? During the 750th anniversary celebrations the year before, the entire district of Kreuzberg had been cordoned off out of fear of violence. How much resistance is possible, what does freedom mean in a walled city? Confrontations, squats, serious riots with the police had occurred time and again in recent years. But this time, the protest had a new dimension. This time, the Senate could not simply restore order and then go back to business as usual. It was condemned to inaction, and on top of that in the very year in which West Berlin wanted to proudly present itself to the world as the first German "City of Culture in Europe." How would the Senate deal with this?

Many West Berliners were on our side. Regular folks drove to the Lenné/Kubat triangle to supply the squatters with food and building materials. While many Western newspapers wrote of "Anarchists" or "Radicals" who challenged the Senate, the state media of the GDR reported only little, and when they did, they spoke of "anti-fascists" and "peace-loving activists". The enemy of my enemy is my friend.

The border guards on the East side watched the action like grandfathers leaning on a pillow and looking out the window, except that in this case the pillow was the top of the wall. As soon as dawn broke, they would sometimes strike up a conversation with the squatters. Once I stood by as a Volkspolizist, a member of the "People's Police" addressed a black-clad couple almost paternally: "From July 1, you can do whatever you want here," he said with a slight Saxon accent, "but now, don't push it!"

Soon, the initially peaceful atmosphere changed. Perhaps it was because more and more activists who were prepared to use violence were setting up camp as well. And also the Senate, legally hobbled, turned to exerting pressure. Police squad cars pulled up next to the triangle. "We are the champions" resounded at full volume from their loudspeakers all night. In response, stones and even explosives flew in the direction of the police. A "true environmentalist needs a watering pot and a rake", West Berlin's mayor Eberhard Diepgen sneered, not "face masks and Molotov cocktails". The police kept arresting people outside the compound, often using their batons.

By now, the village in no man's land became a fortified frontier town where several hundred people had settled. And I came almost daily to monitor what was going on. For Radio 100, the dispute was an important topic. But while I felt first and foremost as a journalist, I also had great sympathy with the squatters. I liked it that they stood in the way of authority, even if their ideological superstructure was unfamiliar to me. I was young, naive, and had only been in the city for two years myself. And even though many of them were very serious about what they were doing, it was also an adventure, a play with fire, an opportunity to thumb their noses at the state.

Then the situation escalated. The squatters dug trenches and built ramparts. The Senate concluded: This is no longer about environmental protection and urban planning, this is a place where enemies of the law are gathering. The police had occasionally fired tear gas already, but on June 18, the situation escalated: water cannons were deployed, tear gas was shot into the area and brought tears to everybody's eyes.

I had just seen on television how police vehicles were gathering and hurriedly made my way to the triangle. When I arrived, I encountered a grotesque situation: While the shiny, new, unmanned monorail rode undaunted above Potsdamer Platz, the adjacent area was shrouded in tear gas. The starry sky was completely invisible. Cartridges with tear gas constantly hit the squatter village, and water cannons drove up and down, covering the huts and tents with their wet, irritant gas-soaked cannonades.

The squatters responded with stones, again. And also the East German border police coughed and scolded—in vain. The bombardment lasted for hours. It felt like war. I walked around the triangle with my recorder to document what was going on until I could hardly see anything. The squatters retreated far to the back of the site, to the Wall that was supposed to protect the triangle. The tear gas did not get that far. However, bad news kept arriving—of broken glass that had not withstood the police water cannon, of burning huts, injured squatters and of enormously frightened chickens and goats.

The West Berlin police were unstoppable. The very next evening they continued their attack, but this time they risked trouble. Not from the squatters, who were checkmated for the time being. But from the GDR: numerous gas cartridges also flew over the Wall. "In the area of the Lenné Triangle, the territory of the GDR is being fired upon," it sounded from the megaphones of the border police, "we demand that you stop this."

Eventually, the political opposition intervened. Walter Momper, then chairman of the Social Democrats, suggested a mediator. The Green-Alternative Rainbow Group in the European Parliament introduced an urgent motion to condemn the use of tear gas as a violation of Article Two of the UN Charter and of the Four-Power Agreement for Berlin. Representatives of the Allied powers in London and Moscow had been in close contact for weeks through their embassies in Bonn and East Berlin. But the GDR was still not considering expelling the squatters itself, as Chairman and General Secretary Erich Honecker himself made abundantly clear at the end of June: "We are surprised ourselves, but the matter will soon be over. Be patient."

As July 1 came closer, West Berlin's many left-wing denizens tried everything they could to prevent the exchange of areas: The Netzwerk Selbsthilfe proposed to East Germany to buy the Lenné Triangle themselves before the handover. The local initiative "Westtangente" and the "Bund für Umwelt- und Naturschutz" demanded that the Senate place the area under nature protection. However, the Senate categorically rejected all demands.

It was at the end of June when squatters started talking about fleeing across the Wall to East Berlin in case the police would try to arrest them. This would be an unheard-of undertaking. Not only I, but many left-wing young adults in the West had been told a hundred times by their conservative parents: "Why don't you go over there if you don't like it here?" However, throwing themselves into the arms of the quite authoritarian GDR was out of the question for most. The fear of ending up in an East German prison without being able to defend ourselves was far too great. We knew that the East Berlin regime was not exactly squeamish in their dealings with rebellious citizens.

But still, the idea kept circulating. Allegedly, the SEW, the West Berlin spin-off of the East German Socialist party, had contacted the authorities in East Berlin. There was also a rumor that the Stasi was involved, but it remained unproven.

In anticipation of imminent eviction, the first squatters took down their tents and dragged their belongings off the grounds in bags, boxes, and shopping carts. Others wanted to stay; they manufactured ladder-like structures and pilfered police barrier fences that were dragged towards the Wall. On the afternoon of June 30, the time had come: the exchange of territory agreed upon between West Berlin and the GDR was to be carried out. The remaining squatters decided that they would simply not leave.

It was very warm that night. At the Lenné Triangle, countless journalists from Germany and abroad were waiting, including me with my recording equipment. Squatters were hanging out together drinking beer, small fires were lit, a group was drumming to keep awake. Midnight came, July 1st dawned—but nothing happened. Rumors buzzed that the site would not be cleared until early morning. Some squatters curled up on the grass to catch some sleep. Others wandered around the compound to stay alert and say their goodbyes. It was as if everyone held their breath for a few hours.

But minutes before five a.m., sat the break of dawn, everyone was abruptly awoken when the police ended the silence: "Dear citizens on the Lenné Triangle," they droned from their loudspeakers, "this area has belonged to West Berlin since midnight. It poses a danger because of the ammunition we suspect is there. Take your belongings and leave the area in the direction of the Brandenburg Gate!"

Police squad cars had arrived overnight, followed by trucks carrying police barricades in addition to mobile water cannons and evacuation vehicles. At 5:15 a.m., the evacuation began. When the first cops stormed the area, the remaining two hundred squatters retreated towards the Wall. In no time at all, they set up their ladders, and after only a few minutes the

first people were sitting on the top of the Wall, including myself. I could see several flatbed trucks rolling up on the east side, loaded with sandbags, escorted by Volkspolizei officers in brown uniforms. They smiled and waved at us. It took only a few moments, then the first squatter courageously jumped into the East. I also wanted to—wanted to be able to report what was happening, at a moment that would surely make history.

But my fellow reporter who had kept watch with me in that night held me back. Clutching my foot, he shouted, “You don’t seriously want to go to the GDR, who knows what they’ll do to you there! You may never come back!” Finally, I gave in and let the others go. And so I know everything that happened in East Berlin only from hearsay: One hundred and eighty-two squatters had chosen to flee to the East. They were provided with breakfast in the main Stasi office and released with the instruction that in the future, they should only enter the GDR territory via the designated border crossings. They were even given subway tickets so that they could return to the West for free.

But I had to stay back and watch, as the West Berlin police unceremoniously and effortlessly removed the barriers set up by the squatters. The cops had not expected such a smooth operation. In an appropriate good mood, they examined the sleeping bags, tents and blankets left behind and began to search the area for ammunition. Meanwhile, a lonely British helicopter circled in the sky. The Kubat Triangle was history.

Martina Schrey, born in 1963, is a staffer at RBB’s Inforadio. She has decades of experience working for radio, TV, print and online media. Her career started at Radio 100, a now-defunct leftwing Berlin station. She is also a trained nurse who was awarded the Christopherus Prize, the author of four books for young people, and a fan of women’s soccer. She has two daughters. *Photo: Dieter Freiberg*

das
zählt

The Caviar Spade

By Wladimir Kaminer

I CAME TO Berlin right after the Wall came down. And ever since I've lived in Berlin, I've gone every week to the Sunday flea market. Although I don't ever really want to buy anything, I always come back home with bags filled with stuff. After a while, I believed I'd figured out why this is: At flea markets, people get hypnotized by things. That's why they move like sleepwalkers, have mist in their eyes, and occasionally act to their own disadvantage. They are psychologically affected by flea market merchandize that is looking for a new owner.

At least I feel that way. If I show interest in something specific and buy, say, a spoon, the entire flea market inventory of cutlery immediately throws itself in my way. Spoons, forks and knives spring up like mushrooms in the fall—and right into my bag.

Once—rather thoughtlessly—I bought a vintage spoon made from aluminum, out of solidarity with my former hometown. It was inscribed in Russian: "Moscow is delighted about every guest". From now on, I could only see cutlery at that flea market. Spoons, forks, knives curled up at every corner. The just-purchased hospitable Moscow spoon looked curiously out of my pocket and gave me well-meaning advice on what else I should definitely buy. Suddenly, I could spot a lot of interesting cutlery—hunter's cutlery, for instance, with the knife and fork fixed with fluffy animal tails. The spoon sported a feather that made it perfect for chicken broth.

Regarding fish cutlery, I had my doubts about whether I actually needed eight oyster forks. We've never eaten eight oysters at once before, and at home, not even one. The Moscow spoon in my pocket commented that it was necessary to have all eight of them. Anyhow, the purchase was inevitable, driven by the mere fact that another associated piece of cutlery that looked like a flat square spoon and adorned with the noble name "caviar spade" could only be bought together with the eight oyster forks.

Due to the freshly formed friendship with the Moscow spoon, I stocked up considerably on my cutlery supplies. I noticed in this process that only foreigners buy cutlery at flea markets. Maybe that's because they come from hungry countries? The locals are probably too disgusted to use secondhand cutlery. On my way back, I bought some dessert spoons decorated with pearls. In addition, I almost bought a mysterious giant fork for large-caliber food, but on closer inspection it turned out to be a brush for back massages.

But I don't need that kind of brush, because I live close to the oldest physiotherapy practice in our district, owned by Mrs. Almert. Mrs. Almert toils from morning till night. She has a lot to do, because most of my neighbors' backs are crooked, strained and hurt like hell somewhere in the middle, usually exactly where a massage brush won't reach anyway. Even as a child, Mrs. Almert had enjoyed massaging her grandma's feet. When asked what she wanted to be when she grew up, she said she wanted to be a foot therapist. And now, she has founded a physiotherapeutic dynasty, together with her daughter.

In her office, patients lie side by side on stretchers, separated by pink curtains. They can't see each other, but they can hear each other. "You tell me when it hurts," Mrs. Almert usually says at the outset. "Is that the point? Is that the point?" She feels her way through the points. I usually lie silently, listening to the voices all around me.

"What is your problem?" Mrs. Almert inquires of a new patient lying to my left.

"I can hear my pulse," the woman replies. "Well, not now, but in the evening, when I sit at home after work, I hear the pulse."

"Do you work in an office? Do you live alone? Is that the point? Is that the point?" Mrs. Almert always correctly guesses where the point of hurt is.

Now she turns to me. "How are you, Mr. Kaminer?"

"Good, as usual. I bought a lot of cutlery, maybe soon I'll write a scientific paper: 'Mental differences in cutlery preferences between natives and immigrants'."

Incidentally, I have since donated the square caviar spade as a display model for an exhibition called "Immigration Germany". The organizers had asked me which items I took with me when I left Russia twenty years ago and what hopes I had associated with Germany.

"I traveled to Germany with almost no luggage, only a caviar spade," I replied. "I had great expectations as far as Germany was concerned, I thought we would be shoveling caviar here every day. Unfortunately, my expectations were not confirmed to this extent."

However, I have kept the aluminum spoon that reads "Moscow is delighted about every guest".

***

Of course, I'm not the only Russian in Berlin. Two of my friends, Katja and Irina, hail from Belarus. They have been studying journalism at Berlin University for two years now. At the same time, they are gaining the required skills for their future journalistic work in a restaurant on Wittenbergplatz as waitresses. The restaurant, a valued West Berlin institution, serves "traditional German cuisine with style" and is never empty. On the large terrace, the last old West Berliners eat their Nuremberg grilled sausages with sauerkraut and then order apple pie with coffee.

Since the Wall came down, however, the pub has been threatened by new, untamed masses of tourists. More and more buses with Berlin travelers stop in front of the place. Guests to the German capital want to taste traditional German cuisine in style. As a result of their excessive interest, this actually decent restaurant is turning more and more into a tourist attraction. Even worse, these strangers want to be constantly entertained; no one is satisfied with a piece of pie or a pair of sausages anymore. For a real Berliner, this is an outrage.

The bulk of the trouble is caused by "those Japanese tourists," the chef often complains. He suspects that they think the restaurant's "traditional German cuisine" is just yet another attraction. And they come in ever new batches and many of them want to be photographed with a serving of pork knuckle, or, as it is called, Eisbein, a classic Berlin dish. They are particularly fascinated by the giant size and gross nature of the pork knuckle. Apparently, the chef has told me more than once, anything gargantuan attracts them.

Usually, the Japanese point their fingers at the plate, loudly shouting

"Ai", which means "Look at that thing" in Japanese. At the same time, they smile enthusiastically into the camera. At that point, my Russian friends Katja and Irina have to take snapshots. In return, they get a good tip, and then the pork knuckle goes back into the kitchen. It has not dawned yet on the Japanese to actually eat the Eisbein. Naturally, the chef is very offended. But just the minute the dish has ended up back in the kitchen, a new portion of pork knuckle is ordered by yet another Japanese to be photographed.

The old West Berliners on the veranda shake their heads at this. "Those foreigners," they keep saying to Katja and Irina, "are they all nuts or what?"

"You have a point," my foreign friends assert, exchanging glances.

Meanwhile, the chef has found a clever solution to salvage his cooking: He created a reusable oversized knuckle of pork that still looks photogenic weeks later. Now, it is always brought out of the kitchen as needed, on a big plate carried by both waitresses. The tourists are happy, and the tips for Katja and Irina have almost doubled.

Still, that didn't make all the problems go away. The other day, a Japanese man came into the restaurant and asked Katja (in English) if he could feed his forty-five children at their restaurant. Katja first thought this was a Japanese tourist joke and just nodded her head in a friendly way. But then they actually came in: forty-five hungry Japanese schoolchildren. They took a seat on the veranda. Their group leader ordered sausage with sauerkraut for all of them, apparently the only words he knew in German. Irina suggested to the group leader that he could feed the children at the take-out next door, but he turned her down. "Sausage and sauerkraut," he kept repeating.

The kitchen had to close for all the other guests and the entire staff of the restaurant was set to work. The Nuremberg sausages in the restaurant are served on huge frying pans. After about an hour and a half, the forty-five pans arrived on the table. "Ai," the Japanese children said in chorus, immediately pulling their cameras out of their backpacks. The white, grease-splattered sausages were photographed frantically from all sides. After that, the kids packed up their cameras again and wanted to order some food. After much toing and froing, the kids left the restaurant, each with a free slice of apple pie in hand.

But now, the chef was left with forty-five pans of sausages and sauerkraut. He was furious. "If anyone orders just one single sausage today, I'll punch them right now," he announced loudly on the porch.

The old West Berliners sitting on the veranda tried to talk some sense into him. "They're just hungry kids, what do they know about cooking," they said.

"Ah, yes," the chef continued to agitate. "Then they should take a few more rice rollmops with them from home before they go on a trip. I'd rather cook for hungry kids from Africa. I'm sure they're not as squeamish as the Japanese."

The chef raged for a while longer, finally downing three Jägermeisters to calm down. Then he went home. The next day, he posted a sign outside, "Cold dishes only today."

It didn't help, the forty-five Japanese children showed up again.

"Oh no, not them again," the chef erupted.

"These are not the ones from yesterday, they're others," Katya and Irina reassured him. And so, still grumbling, he returned to the stove.

***

"Nothing is happening in Charlottenburg," sighed my friend Thomas. A year ago, he acquired a restaurant near Savignyplatz and has been bored to death ever since. Every time I visit him, he tells me how great this place used to be, in good old West Berlin and even before—the only restaurant in town with real Franconian cuisine: boiled blue bockwurst in apple broth and fine wines to go with it. "In the twenties, even charity concerts were held here, and lots of famous musicians performed...Today, only drug-addicted punks come in with their guitars, and even the tourists avoid us and go to East Berlin," Thomas complained.

"East Berlin is cutting edge right now," I nodded.

We were both sat at a corner table, garlands lit up outside, the whole city inexorably transformed into a single Christmas market. The restaurant was empty that evening, with only two retirees sipping their coffee and a young couple discussing their overtly complicated relationship situation. No one was interested in Thomas' blue sausages. Then the door opened—a woman entered the restaurant. She was wearing a long black dress under her coat and a huge hat on her head. It was as if she had fallen out of another era, as if the Komische Opera's costume department had sold off its whole wardrobe just before Christmas.

"I'm hungry," she said to Thomas, "what would you recommend?"

Thomas recommended the blue sausages, of course, along with red wine and plum cake for dessert. The woman in her twenties ate it all, drank another cognac, and then refused to pay. This was the first time something like this had happened to Thomas. While something similar had happened several times already—customers running away without paying their tab—this woman had no intention of running away at all.

"I never pay," she just kept repeating, "I refuse on principle." Thomas was at a loss.

The woman smiled kindly at him and asked if he might have a cigarette for her. He advised her instead, with a scowl, to pay the bill: "Otherwise I'll alert the police."

"Do what you think is right, I never pay," the lady repeated.

Thomas went to the phone, but then returned to the lady: he didn't feel like going to the police. "Think it over carefully, because this can end badly for you," he warned.

"Young man," said the lady "don't yell at me. Alert the whole town for all I care, I'm not running away. Can I have another red wine?"

"What audacity!" Thomas cried in exasperation, and then he called the police after all.

All the guests were now staring at the lady with the hat. She was acting very calmly, as if she did this sort of thing every day. She probably did. One of the retirees gave her a cigarette.

But the police took their sweet time. Thomas became more and more nervous and he ran in pointless circles through his restaurant. Meanwhile, the lady continued to radiate friendliness. Half an hour passed.

"Don't get so upset," she reassured the manager. "They'll come around - sooner or later. The police are busy these days."

"You'd better pay your bill," Thomas replied, "and we'll part as friends."

"Friendship has nothing to do with money," the woman countered. "If we subordinate ourselves to capital and communicate with each other only through bills, we will soon lose what's left of our humanity and sink to animals," she declared, staring at the ceiling.

"That's right," confirmed one of the retirees from the corner, offering the lady another cigarette. "My name is Johannes, by the way," he said.

"But you ate my sausages," Thomas objected. "Just like that! Is that human?"

"I thanked you for it," the woman countered.

Another half hour passed, the police were still not there. "Would you like some red wine, perhaps?" Thomas asked the lady.

"No, I'd rather have a mineral water, but non-carbonated," she said.

Just then the doors opened and a couple of policemen came in. The female policeman took up position at the door, and the male policeman walked up to Thomas.

"Any problems?" he asked. Thomas was sitting at the table with the lady and John the pensioner. They were downing liquor quite fast.

"Sorry, it was a false alarm," he said to the policeman.

"Do you know what a police call-out like this costs?!" the policeman began rambling. "And who will pay for it?"

"I won't pay anything," the lady brought herself back into the conversation. "On principle."

The policeman scolded a bit more, then he and his colleague left the pub. The lady wanted to leave, too. "Come again," Thomas said to her.

"Oh, I don't know about that, maybe next year," she said coquettishly.

"Finally, there is some action in here!" the retirees rejoiced.

Wladimir Kaminer hails from Moscow where he was born in 1967. Since the fall of the Wall, he has lived in Berlin. He has authored more than thirty books, including the bestseller Russendisko *that was turned into a very successful movie. He also produces Kaminer Inside for the public brodcaster 3 SAT. The film series is about traditional cultural venues that showcase modern art. Photo: C. Bertelsmann Verlag*

Achtung!
Sie verlassen
jetzt
West-Berlin

West of Eden

By Harald Jähner

Fittingly, it was the writer Katja Lange-Müller who, coming from the East to the West in 1984, who dramatically summed up the situation of West Berliners after the fall of the Wall: it "pulled their city out from under the ass" of many people. The fall wasn't that deep, but the landing was rough. It was like waking up from a rather bizarre dream. Suddenly the city was flooded with strangers.

Old West Berlin had been an unreal, empty city, especially in the 1970s. Even in the afternoons, there were often only two or three people in the streetcars. The building of the Wall had turned four-lane boulevards into dead ends, where children and dogs played. A gas station in no-man's-land near the Wall in Kreuzberg with no through traffic was left as if from another era; a walled-up stairway was found in a desert of sand, which, according to an information board, had once been called Potsdamer Platz.

A few hundred yards away, a former ballroom loomed out of nowhere. It was inconceivable that one day they would pull it aside on rails to build something around it that would be called the "Sony Center." In many places, you got the feeling that history had taken West Berlin as a pawn: after the war, history first shut down the city until it might later remember what it intended to do with it.

There was silence on the once central squares and streets that were now the outskirts of the city, and in ruins like the Anhalter Bahnhof, where you sometimes thought, if you were sufficiently tipsy, you could still hear the porters calling. As quickly as the wounds of the war in the West German cities had healed, in West Berlin they remained open, if only because of this emptiness.

Convinced Berliners, mostly the newcomers, that is, harbored a kind of pride in their wounds. They saw the city's blatant beat-up state as a true reflection of a reasonable mental state after World War II. Many of the younger West Berliners also found the division to be fair and reasonable, despite all the hardships, while they never tired of dismissing the thoroughly renovated, vital, rival cities of Munich and Hamburg as unfaithful and oblivious to history.

Life on this absurd island was made all the easier as the few sacrifices that had to be made were repaid double and triple-fold. The showcase of the West was generously subsidized. Due to immense tax breaks, it was economically worthwhile to produce fine liqueurs, chocolates, cigarettes, light bulbs, razor blades, motorcycles and turbines even in this inconveniently faraway city.

Life was more leisurely than anywhere else in Germany. It was magical: a big city where you could relax. Everywhere in the craggy urban landscape were havens for allotment dwellers. “Berlin is on a drip feed,” they said; but you have to picture the patient as someone walking along the banks of the Havel River with his IV pole, enjoying the delights of the stimulants streaming through the catheter.

The “bulwark of freedom” also included subsidies for socio-critical art and culture, with which West Berlin demonstrated its liberality. Many thousands of artists and intellectuals made a living from ever new projects, festivals, and exchange programs in some sweet bitterness that knew no curfew and had plenty of birds twittering at dawn.

You walked into the pubs alone and soon found yourself deep in conversation with someone. You didn’t have to bring company with you, as you do today, when you went to the then still very cheap Paris Bar, the Ruine, or the Liliom.

West Berlin was full of unashamed lonely birds, led by the “Widows of Wilmersdorf “, who painted their lips red and expertly dabbed their cheeks. They were accustomed to the excess of women that had characterized Berlin since the last years of the war, as half of the marriageable men perished or were imprisoned.

West Berlin was not a West German city. Its denizens could neither take part in federal elections nor turn to the Federal Constitutional Court; federal politics penetrated the brain of West Berliners only as background noise. Politically responsible for West Berliners were the Western Allies, whose ceremonial farewell in 1990 was greeted with sincere melancholy by a surprising number of people.

Eating oysters at the Café du Lac on Lake Tegel, Scottish haggis, and chicken masala at the annual British Jamboree, spare ribs and enchiladas at the German-American folk festival — long before the globalization of gastronomy, West Berliners could stick their noses into foreign cooking pots. Internationality and provinciality went hand in hand here.

What Golo Mann first dared to say was particularly true for West Berlin: the division of the nation was a great, undeserved good fortune for the Germans, despite all the hardships and some tragedies in detail. Only through the Cold War could the victors of the Second World War become allies within a few years who, at least in the West, were coddled as much as it was possible.

Without the dubious luck of the Cold War, nobody would have reached out for reconciliation to the Germans so quickly after the Holocaust and the crimes of World War II, and Germany would not have been able to return to the global economy. Without the Cold War, Mayor Ernst Reuter would never have been able to call out his “Look upon this city” to the “peoples of the world” during the blockade of West Berlin, at this city that the world had hated and feared like no other four years earlier.

That was in 1948. Nobody could have foreseen at the time that West Berlin’s insane island location could one day become the paradox of a bizarre normality, cemented by a building that meant a prison less for the islanders than for the East Germans on the mainland.

After their former mayor, Willy Brandt, became Chancellor, West Berliners even began to enjoy their somewhat uncomfortable geopolitical situation. The détente policy secured the levees and enabled transit traffic. At the same time, they basked in the continuing interest that the worldwide public had in the island’s illustrious location. Precisely because it was so exposed at the focal point of the East-West conflict, West Berliners could feel protected and safe.

Overprotection and hippie-esque laissez-faire spread throughout the whol city. Berlin’s state politics developed their specific immaturity under the bonnet of very limited responsibilities, which can still be felt today.

It was typical of the island, for example, that Michaele Schreyer of the Green Party, senator for the Environment celebrated a deal with the German Democratic Republic leadership as an ecological success, although it resulted in the unscrupulous dumping of the garbage in Brandenburg. The protests of the East German environmental initiatives went unheeded on the island.

In the end, West Berliners had adapted to the Wall so much that they reacted to its fall like domestic rabbits whose protective walls were suddenly taken away. Of course, the joy that the East Germans had overthrown their government was genuine, but West Berliners reacted reservedly to the suggestion of reunification.

The fear spread that the honorary bear of the West could become a gray mouse of the East. Fear ate up the joy: fear for the peace and quiet in the loveable neighborhoods, fear for a self-determined existence in the shadow of the wall; fear of falling into the middle of a bankrupt country and losing a secure framework of life with the wall.

But then curiosity won out.

Harald Jähner, born in 1953 in the Ruhr region, studied literature, history and art in Freiburg and earned his doctorate in Berlin. He began as a journalist, then headed the press department of the House of World Cultures from 1989 to 1997. At Berliner Zeitung *he headed the art section from 2003 to 2015. Today he is an honorary professor at the University of Fine Arts in Berlin. Photo: Hans Richard Edinger*

Island Time

By Uwe Rada

IF THERE WAS one thing in abundance in West Berlin, it was time. That's why the clocks in the city ticked differently than on the mainland. After the fall of the Wall, I tried to make up for the loss of time with a gain in space.

At some point I had set my mind on this goal. A forty-hour week. A whole work week, only not at work, but at Ex, my favorite pub in Mehringhof, a sprawling courtyard in Kreuzberg inhabited by left-wing enterprises. Almost every evening I was there, meeting with friends; we planned the revolution, drank beer, and got the necessary exercise at punk concerts. If you added up the six days the Ex was open, I had to be there just under seven hours a day – then I would have made it. That would have been a sign. A sign against the pressure of capitalism to be exploited. For a self-determined life. A life without an alarm clock. There was no more radical way to kill time. How ridiculous in comparison was the Union demand for a 35-hour week.

What made West Berlin tick? Above the Europacenter on Breitscheidplatz, a Mercedes star rotated. I don't know how many times it turned on its axis in an hour. It was not important. The star turned, but no time passed. Time stood still. Today, the word "standstill" is associated with the accusation that someone or something is balking at the passage of time, wants to stop it, even turn it back, wants to stand outside of reality. Maybe that's even true.

At that time, we were indeed outside of reality. In West Berlin, the clocks were ticking differently. West Berlin was an island. A plot of land with no space around it. Why should Central European summer or wintertime apply here? Here, island time prevailed.

The other day I was in the city of Havelberg. It's also an island, surrounded by the Havel and its branches before it flows into the Elbe. At the castle uphill, a few young people had gathered. Sat on their mopeds and chatting, they were also silent for some time. They crouched with their arms folded on the handlebars, looking satisfied. Picked their noses. Shooed a wasp away. Did not ponder what they had done during the day. Didn't waste a thought on when they had to get home. Pushed their mopeds back a few feet to get the last rays of sun. They were just there. I was envious.

I wonder if they would remember this moment later. Are we more likely to remember doing nothing or being busy? Once, I took the city bus to Dreilinden, the checkpoint at the Western edge of Berlin and stood at the border with my thumb up. Didn't want to visit my parents, just out. Away from the island. Through the GDR to the mainland. Get out and walk through the Lapp Forest, just behind the border dividing East and West Germany. Getting some air. Seeing no people. When I hitchhiked back in the evening, I was satisfied. That evening I didn't go to the Mehringhof, but rather to bed early.

Trips like the one to the Lapp Forest were rare. Mostly, I was just there, like the others who were also just there. I met them at rallies, communal meetings, at the Kiezpalaver. Sometimes, we squatted on the sidewalk in front of Café Jenseits at Heinrichplatz in Kreuzberg and watched passers-by. When we ran out of beer, one of us got up and went to the kiosk, the others continued to hang out. Picked their noses. Shooed away a wasp. Didn't think about what they had done during the day. They were just there. I wasn't jealous then. Back then, that was how it was.

I don't think there was this daytime and nighttime in West Berlin as we know it today. There was no after-work hours anyway, because there was no work like we do it today. When I was penning my novel *1988*, a love story between Jan from Kreuzberg, and Wiola from Krakow, I was pondering about how the mood in West Berlin was different from today. I noted:

"I think you can maybe describe it as: nothing happens unaware anymore, not a path you take, not a thought you think. In those days, you didn't race through the landscape, it passed you by. It was the same with our story. It passed us by, it drew us into itself, it told itself. We were not the authors of this story, but its characters.

Today, anyone who isn't the all-wise narrator of their story entitled 'My Own Life' is considered not to have made it. Someone who can't find his way, who can't get along with the inexorable rhythm of time, this drumming that some mistake for life. Basically, he is a loser who has lost the thread of his life. In those days, not everyone had to be a writer, and only those who were worrying about their careers needed a thread in their lives. Everyone else was drifting and accepted every detour as a gift. Did we have more time back then? Did we think we would live endlessly? Or did we just manage to dive deeper into this life, not wanting to master it, but just surrendering to it?"

I also wrote in *1988*, the novel, that sometimes, we went to the wall like we go to the sea today. Just to see if everything was still there. There it was again, the island, with its island thoughts. Its island time that had no sense of time. Not to mention the space. An island does not need space around its shores. The only important issues were the border crossings and the directions they pointed to: Hamburg in the northwest, Hanover and Cologne in the west, Nuremberg and Munich in the south. I had not heard of the east at that time.

I came to the island from the Southwest. It was April 1983. I was planning to enroll at Freie Universität, the deadline was tight. My mother had given me the money for a plane ticket and for a boarding house on Kurfürstendamm. The landlady of the boarding house was gruff. A parrot sat on her shoulder and made gruff sounds. She pressed a key with two endings into my hand. It was a key for the front gate, not uncommon for pre-war buildings in West Berlin at that time. When I glanced at it, puzzled, she rolled her eyes and left me standing. I felt as if I had stepped into a movie from the Fifties, black and white, gloomy-melancholic, the outcome uncertain.

In one of the side streets of Kurfürstendamm I found a phone booth and called my mother. While I was on the phone, I saw a car drive around the corner way too fast, almost hitting a pedestrian. The pedestrian whacked the hood with his fist. The driver got out, hopping mad. The pedestrian pulled a spray can out of his pocket and sprayed something in the driver's face. I think I reported everything to my mother, without thinking about it, in real time. Live feed from a West Berlin phone booth. The next day I went to Freie Universität, enrolled, got on the waiting list for a dormitory, then drove to the Zoo train station. When I asked a passer-by how to get to the airport, he shook his head. Take the train, he advised me, planes cause too much dirt.

Nevertheless, I left the island via Tegel airport. The next time I came by car. It didn't take long before I was one of the islanders myself.

Later, I wondered whether I had become like the first-person narrator in Nicolas Born's novel *Die erdabgewandte Seite der Geschichte*, *The History of the Averted Side of the Earth*. Born's story about a failing, failed writer was the first island book I read on the island, once, twice, over and over. His hero is a searching, suffering, disgruntled self who has lost all sense of time. "If passing time shines through in the book at all," Born's friend Peter Handke wrote in a review, "it is only in the form of changing seasons: behind the fierce day and night actions (or paralyses) of people the leaves fall, the hazy mist of early winter breaks in, and then the foliage on the trees is already so dark again."

Such a book, I think, could only be written in West Berlin. Time in abundance, standstill, dead time, that was the humus from which an ego could form, but also lose itself again. But without time, there are not even these two possibilities.

Did I read Born again and again because he, like Handke, was a representative of the so-called new inwardness? Back then, I would have said no, would have referred to my political irreconcilability with the political system, to the marches and activities in the hood. Today, I'm not so sure. The escape into politicking is probably nothing else than the counter to a forty-hour drinking week in the Mehringhof. They were both at the averted side of the earth.

What has remained of island life is my view of the backsides, the shadowy sides, the stories from the averted sides of the earth, in our cities. Or as Nicolas Born put it in one of his poems.

With us, history breaks up.
You can see it most clearly when the train
slowly runs along the backsides of the cities
warehouses, courtyards, where the laundry is inside out
and the flowery windows
the averted side of the history.

Loneliness and the attraction to death also were part of the island. When I squatted in a house at Reichenberger Strasse 63a with a few comrades in November 1987, it was bitterly cold. We climbed into the vacant tenement via the neighboring rooftop. But those roofs were full of ice. To get to our destination, we had to cross not only very slippery flat roofs, but also a steep gable roof. With our left foot we stepped on the gable roof, while our right foot was placed on a board parallel to the roof and a few inches below. To my right, the abyss opened up and I felt a pull into the depths like I never had before. One wrong step, one slip, and it was all over. Sweet temptation, death. And yet, I already suspected, we hadn't even learned to live yet. Or had we?

We did make it. Right after we had managed to climb the roof of Reichenberger 63a, we could hear that the police were already in the building. Some of us now wanted to go back. I said, "you can go if you want, but I'm staying. I'd rather go to jail than climb this roof again." Since that day on the roofs of the island I am no longer free from the fear of heights. Not even on the mainland, with solid ground under my feet.

One part of living on the island was the island dream. I don't know why, but it kept coming back time and again. Once, I got on the U7 subway at Mehringdamm station, to Rudow. Somewhere behind Britz-Süd, the unimaginable happened. In the darkness of the tunnel, the subway left its original route to disappear on a side rail behind an invisible wall, just like in Alice in Wonderland or on Platform 9 ¾ at King's Cross in

Harry Potter. Had this subway been hijacked? Or was it just that no one had ever discovered this switch and rail? Before I could think about it in my dreams, the train pulled out of the tunnel again. Out of the windows, the Alps appeared. We drove along a creek through dreamy, beautiful villages with geraniums on wooden balconies. It was probably a phantom pain that produced this dream. An island malaise. A longing for the mainland. The time I still had in abundance was no longer enough. Rather, now something new announced itself – the space.

I had looked for the mainland earlier already. Again and again we had left the island, crossed over, in the direction of Hamburg and Helmstedt, and then on to another island, perhaps Amrum, or Paris or Copenhagen, cities where there was as much island life as in West Berlin, although they were surrounded by mainland.

I remember going to Paris once with a friend, and we almost challenged geography itself. In Berlin, we made a bet on whether we would be able to walk through the city from north to south, from périphérique to périphérique. But we cheated and went to the little town of Deauville instead, at the English Channel. We went swimming, paying no attention to the tide, and were lucky to lose only our shoes and not our lives. Barefoot, I stepped on a broken piece of glass. Back on the West Berlin island, I told everybody that we got footsore because it was so far to walk from the north of Paris to the south. We let the Deauville adventure go unmentioned. Perhaps because it would have awakened the longing to be able to travel from Kreuzberg to Ahlbeck on the Baltic Sea. Or did we not know about Ahlbeck at that time?

In my novel *1988*, Wiola broke into Jan's life, but one could also say that space broke into time. Jan did not know much about Krakow, nor did he know that Poland was about to change for quite some time, while in Berlin things continued to be at a standstill. But the first waves were crashing onto the shores of the island, leaving not only fictional characters like Wiola stranded, but also people of flesh and blood; ethnic German immigrants from Russia who arrived at the end of 1988 or the beginning of 1989, Polish merchants who transformed Potsdamer Platz all the way to Reichpietschufer into a Polish outdoor market. A storm was brewing right in front of the island.

Now that the storm has passed, has dissipated, I find it difficult to find the traces of my old island life. The real places are still there, but they no longer breathe that sense of life, are no longer timeless as they were in island times, but rather fast-moving. Often, the names of the pubs and the stores change faster than the year.

The time of the island is over. But what we got in its place still exists; the connection to the mainland. West Berlin is no longer surrounded by the GDR, but by Brandenburg (and East Berlin), and other borders have opened up as well. In the novel *1988*, Jan had to apply for a visa to travel to Krakow with Wiola. But today I just go. I don't travel to Paris and Copenhagen that often anymore. I'd much rather go to the east. It almost seems to me that space has taken the place of time. But both, I already suspect, are limited resources. After the side of history facing the earth has taken time and invaded the backyards to modernize them, it will now also infiltrate the last corners of the formerly inaccessible terra incognita.

Do I still long for the island? Of course, but I didn't want to live there anymore. Are there still many spaces on the mainland that I have not yet discovered? Of course, but others have long since discovered them before me.

Am I a mainlander now? I'll have to think about it. For more than a year now, I've also been living in the Schlaubetal, a valley near the Polish border. I'm in Germany's most eastern nature park, in a house by the wayside. But still. The nearest train station is only a hundred yards away.

Postscript: No, I don't know whether I actually managed the forty-hour week in the Ex. But the pub in Kreuzberg's Mehringhof is still ingrained in my memory. That's one of the reasons why I sent Jan and Wiola, the heroes of my book *1988*, to this place, so that they could get to know each other. But that's another story.

Uwe Rada, born in Göppingen in 1963, is a reporter at the daily paper taz *and an author. His focus is on urban development and Eastern Europe. He has written three books about three European rivers, the Oder, Memel and Elbe. In 2017 his debut novel* 1988 *was published by Edition Fototapeta. Rada has lived in West Berlin since 1983 and in Grunow, Brandenburg, since 2019. Photo: Marko Cerovac*

The Socialist Paradise

By Eva C. Schweitzer

THIRTY-FIVE YEARS ago, a socialist paradise perished almost without a trace. An actual socialist paradise, not a "really existing" one *real existierend,* as East Germany boasted itself, which sounded satirical even then but wasn't. That paradise existed on its own island where everyone could live according to their needs. We did not have to work. Instead, we could talk about socialism or art all day. We were living in true solidarity, spending our time cleaning the backyard together or barbecuing on the roof of some old tenements, with cheap beer and dirt-cheap rents. Sure, those apartments had coal heating and no running warm water. But who cares when the only obligation is one class at the university (per week), and when you could visit a city-run bathhouse rented by the hour?

It was a paradise with no draft, no army (except those of the Western Allies, which you didn't notice much if you always stayed in Kreuzberg), and no private ownership of the means of production. In fact, there was no production, as there were no factories except for Schering, Philip Morris, and Mercedes. And these were heavily subsidized by West Germany. But the pubs never closed, and our biggest problem was that a makeshift farm near the Wall didn't grow enough grass to feed the mountain goats imported from Nicaragua. We are talking, of course, about West Berlin.

West Berlin was the bigger half of the former capital of the fallen Third Reich, occupied after World War II - but it quickly considered itself liberated. This half morphed into a capitalist showcase for the West in the middle of the East. Or at least it was supposed to morph, because at first, about a million West Berliners gradually packed their bags and settled someplace else; in the Harz mountains, Hamburg, or a Bavarian village. They brought their dialect with them, which was considered funny (my father, a Berliner, was once asked in a bakery in Bavaria whether he wanted Schrippen, an effort of the locals to be nice by using the Berlin term for bread rolls, even though that sounds really odd to Bavarian ears). Many of them reveled in their memories for the rest of their lives.

Meanwhile, West Berlin filled up with students, refugees from the Bundeswehr, feminists, wannabe artists, early green activists, and members of communist splinter groups protesting the Vietnam War, Ronald Reagan and the military-industrial complex. They lived on student loans they didn't intend to repay, and something called the Berlinzulage. This was an eight-percent add-on on wages—and yes, students got Berlin allowance, too. They also saved on rent by squatting in buildings which belonged—like practically all housing—to the City of Berlin. These were more like abandoned housing projects, but it still felt like fighting capitalism.

House squatting was a bit like renting from the municipal housing administration in East Berlin, except that our apartments were eventually renovated with lots of government money. And, of course, there were all those subsidized clubs, associations, and political groups where you could also spend big chunks of your life.

The housing, the Berlinzulage, the easy money, where did all that dough come from? I have no idea. Did it come from the sparkling wine tax? Gas tax? VAT? Donations? Lottery tickets? Somebody must have paid for it. Presumably, the money came from West Germany, Wessiland, as we called the Federal Republic we had left behind. And it didn't just go to students so they could sleep late or get politically involved instead of slaving away in part-time jobs. The Senate—the city government—became the largest employer with massive infusions of federal aid.

The Senate and its municipal subsidiaries (the energy providers Bewag and Gasag, the BVG transportation authority, and the BSR garbage collection agency, among others) employed about half a million West Berliners, more than half of the total workforce. There were more than twice as many district offices as today, all well-staffed. Only the Turks—who had also come to West Berlin in the hundreds of thousands—worked at Schering, Philip Morris, and Mercedes, and they often looked a little lost and were probably freezing.

At that time, I lived in Chamissoplatz, a beautiful turn-of-the-century quarter, one of the few that had survived World War II, now a designated urban redevelopment area. I was volunteering for the Mieterrat, the local Tenants Council. Once, the city commissioned us to research the population of one city block. We found that one-third of the inhabitants were students, one-third were retirees, and only one-third worked. The retirees were all old Berliners who had not made it out in time and now grumbled about the students, "those bums." The students mainly came from West Germany and felt like they were spearheading the revolution. The workers were all from Turkey and were the only ones with money.

The city of Berlin also owned commercial buildings where left-wingish projects tinkered away, kept afloat by the aforementioned Berlinzulage. At that time, I worked at a small, left-wing newspaper, let's call it *taz, die tageszeitung*, which survived mainly due to its managing director's talent, exploiting the many tax write-offs in West Berlin that ordinary mortals had no idea existed (thanks, Kalle!). Once, I got a call for help from a guy who worked for a project of hard-to-describe provenance. The project faced a rent increase from 3.67 to 4.24 Deutschmarks—or something like that. Turns out they had the same municipal landlord as us, the newspaper! I had a nice phone conversation with the head of said municipal landlord, and he assured me that they had a pretty, pretty, pretty good relationship with all their commercial tenants. Also with us, of course. "And it would be a shame if something happened to that beautiful relationship," my boss, Thomas Rogalla remarked afterwards.

In short, we were all one big family in West Berlin. We had left-wing, alternative radio stations, locksmith stores run by butch women, neighborhood magazines with unpaid staff working at nights, left-wing printing plants, political bicycle repair stores, revolutionary pubs, gay bars, semi-gay bars, mixed gay bars, lesbian cultural centers, anti-fascist summer universities, and an entire "Alternative Party" with four or five wings. Instead of well-kept English-style parks, we had wild plants growing behind fences on defunct railroad tracks that had once led to Königsberg and Danzig. Television didn't start until noon (I think, since I was not awake that early). No one was awake that early anyway, except the Turks, and they were watching Turkish TV with satellite dishes. Or were actually at work.

Of course, West Berlin had its highlights, colorful, twinkling lights, at least once a year when the Berlinale Film Festival opened. The Berlinale offered real jobs, many of which went to students or former students (if they hadn't nabbed a job as an adjunct at Free University or with the city government). Unsurprisingly, the Berlinale was also subsidized, but it was worth it! It showcased revolutionary films and political documentaries, and the occasional minor scandal.

The Berlinale was not as polished as Cannes or Hollywood, but still,

it gave West Berlin glamour, unlike the dreary half-town next door. We only entered the eastern part occasionally, mostly when SEW, an offshoot of the communists, sponsored a trip where the usual entrance visa fee of twenty-five Deutschmarks was waived, and we could drink cheap beer for peanuts (i.e., East German marks). But why go at all? West Berlin had pubs, bars, and clubs on every corner. No closing time! Did I mention that? And the cheap beer? The waiters also got Berlinzulage.

Somehow, we never saw the Wall. The other day, browsing through my old photos, I found precisely three pictures of the Wall. Yet, I had practically worked in its shadow, some ten meters from Checkpoint Charlie, for years. Subsequently, we refused to believe in the fall of the Wall—and not just the Left. At the biggest daily newspaper after

Springer, let's call it *Tagesspiegel*, the phone rang on that famed evening of November 11, shortly before eleven o'clock. An excited reader shouted into the phone that the Wall was open! Masses of East Berliners were streaming into the West, right now! Unbelievable! The night-shift editor on duty, already half out the door, told the man to stop the crazy talk and hung up. At least the *taz* was aware of the fall of the Wall, but then again it was located right at Checkpoint Charlie.

The fall of the Wall wrought disaster within the socialist paradise. Helmut Kohl sang the West German national anthem from the tower of the Rathaus Schöneberg, the West Berlin City Hall—our city hall, the scene of countless sit-ins, protests, and demonstrations! The federal government cut Berlin aid faster than a Taliban could shoot down a Soviet helicopter. The public administration job pool was frozen, only temporarily mitigated because East Berlin desperately needed West Berlin civil servants (or so we thought). Next came the job cuts. The number of district offices was halved. This was accompanied by slash-and-burn funding cuts for leftwing alternative projects, which were the heart and soul of West Berlin.

In the meantime, I had moved on to the above-mentioned, not-quite-leftist *Tagesspiegel*, whose managing director was also well-versed in tax law, albeit not as well as Kalle. A colleague drew our attention to a major scandal, a canary in the coal mine, so to speak, or the harbinger of an avalanche. Shockingly, the Senate wanted to cut off funding to an important political entity, a group of lesbian alcoholics who were members of the hard-left part of the Antifa movement called the "Autonome" or "black bloc." Previously they had received 400,000 marks a year; what for was not entirely clear, but who cares? Anyhoo, the money was gone, or rather, it was now been spent elsewhere, probably in the East, where they were still recovering from the *really existing socialism.*

Berlin did have a strong Antifa presence, but even at the best of times, there were, at most, 10,000 people in the black-clad bloc. Maybe 3,000 were women, fewer than ten percent of whom were lesbians. Probably ten percent of those drank. That comes to about 10,000 Deutschmarks per group member. You can buy a lot of beer with that! (Especially at West Berlin prices.) But beer prices were rising as well, along with the rents. And the number of jobs from privately-owned means of production were finally rising from tiny to noticeable.

Next, the Bundestag decided to move the nation's capital from Bonn to Berlin. The spirited debate in the German parliament went on for hours and was broadcast live on television. After the vote was cast—it was already past midnight—I called my father in Bavaria, the born Berliner, and I was trembling with excitement and enthusiasm.

"Dad! Dad! Berlin will be the capital! How wonderful!"

My father, scowling, "Good God, that's gonna cost us another bundle! How could they!" I was shocked and horrified because he, the Berliner, wanted to keep boring Bonn as the capital. He was shocked and horrified because I, the left-wing dreamer, liked the idea of Berlin becoming mighty again. So, the demise of the socialist paradise tore whole families apart (temporarily).

Oh, my West Berlin. Where the city center was filled with garden allotments, war ruins in disrepair and 24/7 pubs. Where we stole wooden planks from construction sites to cut them up and burn them instead of spending money on coal, with a saw also stolen from a construction site. The city where we didn't go to a department store to buy a coffee machine, but debated in the weekly group meeting of the lesbian autonomous alcoholics collective whether anyone knew anyone who had a coffee machine to spare, because why would an alcoholic need coffee? The city where an Atari desktop with no hard drive was the epitome of bourgeois luxury. The city whose young denizens went to the Dreilinden border checkpoint, the main hitchhiking point, hoping for a tourist to load us into their cars to visit home for Christmas. Because, unlike the East Germans, we were free to travel. At home, we listened to our parents complaining that West Berlin would cost so much. If only they had known back then how things would develop!

Ah, our West Berlin! The only socialist paradise that ever worked! All it took was massive federal help and plenty of free cash! On November 9, 1989, it ceased to exist. For a little while, there were still a few pockets of resistance, like the endless construction site of the new airport and, of course, the Berlinale. Who knows when the city will be entirely plowed under by capitalism, but it can't be much longer. Here's to latte macchiato!

Eva C. Schweitzer moved from Munich to West Berlin in 1982, where she studied at the FU and wrote for the taz *and* Tagesspiegel. *Today, she lives in Berlin and New York, where she did her dissertation. She writes for* Kleine Zeitung, Cicero *and* Baumeister *and has published twelve books, most recently* Links Blinken, Rechts Abbiegen (*Westend, Frankfurt*). *She also runs the Berlinica publishing house. Photo: Thilo Rückeis*

PICTURE CREDITS

The First Brick in the Wall
P. 8: Berliners are fleeing the Wall at Bernauer Strasse (public domain); p. 11: Nightclub Resi in the 1920s (historic postcard).

The Day When Kennedy Came
P. 14: Kennedy and Willy Brandt at Checkpoint Charlie (Landesarchiv Berlin); p. 16: Presidential convoy to Rathaus Schöneberg; p. 19: nearby roof (all Bundesarchiv).

Christmas Rituals
P. 23: The author and her mother in front of their Christmas tree (private); p. 24: Christmas candles in a window (Eva C. Schweitzer).

The Course from Air
P. 28: The old hangar at Tempelhof with a PanAm airliner (Landesarchiv Berlin); p. 30: airliner in the sky; p. 31: the tower of Tempelhof; p. 32: a candy bomber at the Deutsches Technikmuseum in Berlin (all Eva C. Schweitzer).

The Blue Angel is Coming Home
P. 34: Marlene Dietrich in *The Blue Angel* (public domain); p. 37, Marlene's gravestone; p. 38: A plaque at 65 Leberstrasse (Eva C. Schweitzer).

Little America
P. 40: Sharona Zuriel on her first day at school (private); p. 43: the Outpost Cinema; p. 44 Halloween candy (all Eva C. Schweitzer).

Kids of Kreuzberg
P. 49: The author at Lohmühleninsel (private); p. 50: children in Kreuzberg; p. 53: the riot of May 1, 1987; p. 54: girls at a streetfair (all Eva C. Schweitzer).

Prison Wine
P. 59: Rudi Dutschke at a rally with comrades (Bundesarchiv); p. 60: Rudi-Dutschke-St. in Kreuzberg (Eva C. Schweitzer); p. 63: Gretchen Dutschke (private).

Pretty Sigi and The Skyscraper
P. 70: Klaus Schütz and Sigrid Kressmann-Zschach (Landesarchiv Berlin); p. 73: Willy Kressman-mural at a soccer stadium in Kreuzberg (Eva C. Schweitzer); p. 76: topping-out of the Kreisel on September 15, 1972 (Landesarchiv Berlin).

From Wedding to Wilmersdorf
P. 80: Wedding, Badstrasse (Eva C. Schweitzer); p. 82: Erkan Arikan as a child (private); p. 85: Geisbergstrasse in Wilmersdorf (Eva C. Schweitzer).

The Trek of the Draft Resisters
P. 90: Checkpoint Charlie (Landesarchiv); p. 93: An American jeep at the Alliiertenmuseum in Zehlendorf (Eva. C. Schweitzer).

Transit to Wessiland
P. 98: A short break at Transit Autobahn; p. 101: a sign at the border; p. 104: Zoo train station (all Landesarchiv Berlin); p. 107: Tanja Dückers as a child in Berlin (Alexander Dückers)

Adventures in Plänterwald
P. 110: a ride at Plänterwald (Landesarchiv Berlin).; p. 112, 115, 116: visitors at the Kreuzberger Festliche Tage fair in the 1980s (Eva C. Schweitzer).

Heros on Hauptstrasse
P. 118: A plaque for David Bowie at his former house at 155 Hauptstrasse; p. 121: A plaque for Christopher Isherwood at 17 Nollendorfstrasse; p. 122: A transit visa for Christiane F. (from *Die Allerallerschönsten Interviews von Wolfgang Müller*, Martin Schmitz Verlag, 1989; we thank Wolfgang Müller); p. 126: Romy Haag (Landesarchiv Berlin); p. 129: Bowie during a Berlin appearance (Wikipedia).

Willi Schulz and the Bang Chamber
P. 132; Kuckuck, a squatted building in Kreuzberg behind a sign for an art exhibit; p. 137: a squatted house in Kreuzberg; p. 138: a protest sign against slumlords; P 141: the old water tower at Gleisdreieck (all Eva C. Schweitzer).

Survival in Berlin
P. 148: Victoria on the Siegessäule (Eva C. Schweitzer); p. 151: Ulrike Buschbacher, Claudia Steinberg, and Anna Steegmann in a NYC subway car (Rosa von Praunheim); p. 152: Gay Pride in Berlin (Eva C. Schweitzer).

The Ghost Train
P. 154: Anhalter Bahnhof; p. 156, 159, 160, 162: deserted Gleisdreieck area and Yorckbrücken in the 1980s (Eva C. Schweitzer).

Wannsee Beach
P. 164: a beach chair at Wannsee (Landesarchiv Berlin); p. 167: the Wannsee entrance (Eva C. Schweitzer); p. 168: Wannsee in 1926 (Bundesarchiv).

Architects and Tanks
P. 179: a piece of the Berlin Wall in Battery Park City, New York (Eva C. Schweitzer); p. 174: American tanks on Bismarckstrasse (Stars&Stripes). P. 176, 177: the strike of architectural students in 1978 (Hans-Peter Achatzi).

Foundling Bird
P. 182, 185, 186, 189: crows and pigeons in Berlin (Eva C. Schweitzer).

Squatting in No-Mans-Land
P. 190, 193, 194: the Berlin Wall, p. 201: a rally at Kurfürstendamm (all Eva C. Schweitzer); p. 198: a flyer about the Kubat-triangle (Landesarchiv Berlin).

The Caviar Spade
P. 202: fleamarket in the Street of 17. Juni (Eva C. Schweitzer).

West of Eden
P. 210: a border sign in front of the Brandenburg Gate (Bundesarchiv); p. 213: East Side Gallery (Eva C. Schweitzer).

Island Time
P. 216: Gleisdreieck, p. 221: the Slumberland pub (all Eva C. Schweitzer).

The Socialist Paradise
P. 227: rooftop in Kreuzberg, p. 228: graffiti (all Eva C. Schweitzer)

Sebastian Ringel
Leipzig!
Softcover; $24.95, 224 pages
6.7x9.5", 224 pictures b/w & color
ISBN: 978-1-935902-59-1

Cornelia Dömer
Martin Luther's Travel Guide
Softcover; $13.95, 176 pages
5x8", 140 full color pics & maps
ISBN: 978-1-935902-44-7

Lothar Heinke
Wings of Desire
Softcover; $16.95, 102 pages
7.5x9.25", 123 pictures full color
ISBN: 978-1-935902-14-0

Michael Brettin
Berlin 1945
Softcover; $24.95, 218 pages
8.5x11",177 pictures b/w
ISBN: 978-1-935902-02-7

Kurt Tucholsky

Berlin! Berlin!

Dispatches from the Weimar Republic

Kurt Tucholsky
Berlin! Berlin!
Softcover; $14.00, 208 pages
5.5x8.5", 41 pictures b/w
ISBN: 978-3-960260-27-1

Kurt Tucholsky
Germany? Germany!
Softcover; $15.00, 208 pages
5.5x8.5", 6 b/w pictures
ISBN: 978-1-935902-38-9

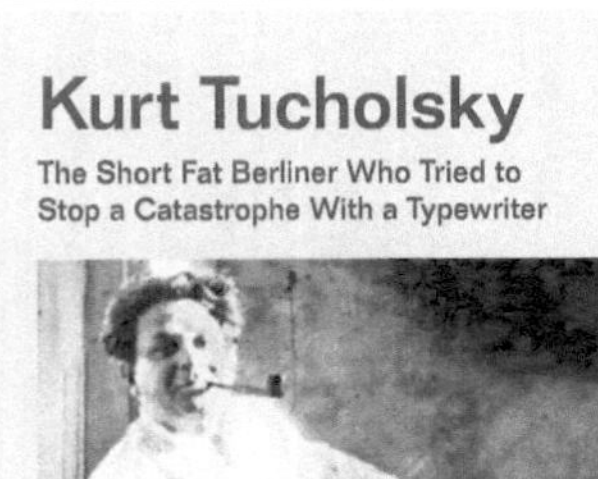

Harold Poor
Kurt Tucholsky
Softcover; $19.95, 256 pages
6x9", 21 pictures b/w
ISBN: 978-1-935902-47-8

Kurt Tucholsky
Prayer After The Slaughter
Softcover; $12.95, 116 pages
5x8", 6 b/w pictures
ISBN: 978-1-935902-28-7

Kurt Tucholsky
Rheinsberg
Hardcover; $12.95, 96 pages
5x8", 26 pictures color & bw
ISBN: 978-1-935902-25-6

Kurt Tucholsky
Hereafter
Hardcover; $12.95, 96 pages
5x8", 23 color pictures
ISBN: 978-1-935902-89-8

Donna Swarthout
A Place They Called Home
Hardcover; $19.95, 208 pages
6x9",12 pictures b/w
ISBN: 978-1-935902-65-2

Nachama, Schoeps, Simon
Jews in Berlin
Softcover; $26.95, 310 pages
6x9", 372 pictures b/w & color
ISBN: 978-1-935902-60-7

Monika Märtens
Berlin for Free
Softcover, 8x5"; $10.95
104 pp, over 100 addresses
ISBN: 978-1-935902-40-9

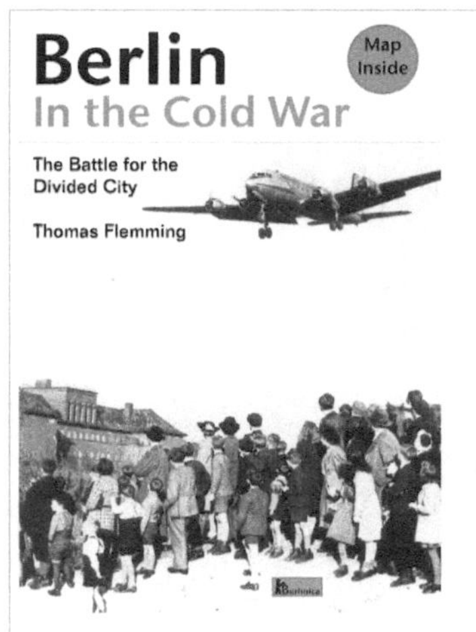

Thomas Flemming
Berlin in the Cold War
Softcover, $10.95, 90 pages
6.7x9.5"; 54 pics & maps b/w
ISBN: 978-1-935902-80-5

Ernst Toller
Hinkemann. A Tragedy
Softcover; $11.95, 86 pages
Dimensions: 5x8"
ISBN: 978-1-935902-52-2

Ernst Toller
Hoppla, We're Alive!
Softcover, $13.95, 144 pages
Dimensions: 5x8"
ISBN: 978-1-935902-49-2

Rose Marie Donhauser
The Berlin Cookbook
Softcover, $15.00, 104 pages
8.5x8.5"; 60 Recipes
ISBN: 978-3-960260-5-47

Michael Cramer
The Berlin Wall Today
Softcover, $15.95, 102 pages
8.5x8.5"; 174 pics/maps full color
ISBN: 978-1-935902-10-2

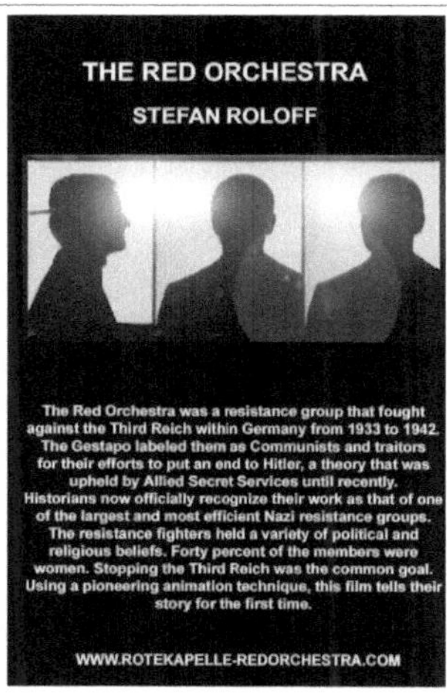

Stefan Roloff
The Red Orchestra
Documentary on Movie DVD
Runtime 57 min; $24.95
English with German subtitles

The Path To Nuclear Fission
The Story of Lise Meitner and Otto Hahn

A Documentary by Rosemarie Reed
Narrated by Linda Hunt
DVD

Rosemarie Reed
The Path to Nuclear Fission
Documentary on Movie DVD
Runtime 81 min; $19.95
English with German subtitles

Walter Hasenclever/Kurt Tucholsky
Christopher Columbus
Softcover, $14.95, 160 pages
Dimensions: 5x8"
ISBN: 978-1-935902-09-6

Egon Erwin Kisch
Paradise America
Softcover, $24.95, 320 pages
6x9"; 42 pictures b/w
ISBN: 978-1-935902-00-3

Alfred Kerr
New York and London
Softcover; $13.95,168 pages
Dimensions: 5.5x8.5"
ISBN: 978-1-935902-31-7

Alexander Roda Roda
Springtime in America
Softcover; $12.95,136 pages
Dimensions: 5.5x8.5"
ISBN: 978-1-935902-01-0

www.ingramcontent.com/pod-product-compliance
Lightning Source LLC
Chambersburg PA
CBHW051306210726
48287CB00002B/691